DICTIONARY
OF PROBLEM WORDS
FOR STUDENTS OF ENGLISH

EUGENE J. HALL

MINERVA BOOKS, LTD.

137 West 14th Street, New York, NY 10011

Published by
MINERVA BOOKS, LTD.
137 West 14th Street
New York, NY 10011

PRINTED IN THE UNITED STATES OF AMERICA

ISBN: 0-8056-0125-2

INTRODUCTION

Many of the words and expressions that a native speaker of a language takes for granted may present the greatest difficulties for a student trying to learn that language. They are often words or expressions that are among the most frequently used, indeed so common that native speakers will not be able to define them and even fail to understand why anyone could have trouble with them.

The words that present problems for students of English differ from language to language, but in general they fall into several distinct groups. First of all, there are function words — words that have a primarily grammatical rather than a semantic purpose. Among the function words that cause particular difficulties for students of English are the determiners — the high frequency words that classify nouns as identified or unidentified, nearer or farther, enumerated or quantified.

As a further complication, the determiners sometimes *do* have special meanings in addition to their grammatical function. It was a Brazilian teacher of English who once pointed out to me that until she went to school in the United States, no one had ever taught her nor had she ever seen in a textbook the use of *some* as an expression of enthusiasm or awe, as in "That was some storm last night!"

The intensifiers, the little words like *very* that strengthen — or sometimes weaken — the adjectives and adverbs with which they are used, also cause problems for many students of English. The shades of meaning of these words, say between *very good* and *too good*, or between *very good* and *pretty good*, are often difficult for students to grasp.

Prepositions, the high-frequency words that introduce adjectival or adverbial phrases, often differ from language to language. English-speaking students of Spanish, for example, usually have difficulty with *por* and *para*, while speakers of Spanish — and several other languages as well — have special problems with *in*, *on*, and *at* when learning English. Prepositions have been covered in a previous publication in this series, *Dictionary of Prepositions for Students of English*, but *in*, *on*, *at*, and a few others which are consistently troublesome are discussed again in this book.

3

Another problem arises when there is a single word in one language with meanings that will be expressed by two or more words in another. To use Spanish as an example again, speakers of English have extraordinary difficulty distinguishing between *ser* and *estar* since in English the one verb *to be* expresses the meanings of both the Spanish verbs. In English, the pairs *do* and *make, borrow* and *lend*, and *say* and *tell* cause similar problems for speakers of many other languages. Another somewhat similar difficulty arises when the pattern for words of equivalent meaning differs from language to language, as with the English verb *to like*, which reverses the structure used with its equivalents in several other languages.

This book tries to provide help on these and several other words and expressions that classroom practice has shown are frequent problems for students of English. The words are presented both semantically and structurally; that is, both their meanings and the patterns in which they are used are discussed and then illustrated with a number of examples that put the problem words and expressions into a context that will make it easier for the students to understand them. The example sentences are especially important, since many of the words covered in this book are so common that they can be defined only in less common terms.

This book is not primarily a grammar, but in three cases words with similar grammatical uses are grouped together — demonstratives, possessive forms, and relative pronouns — because the words in those categories have similar functions and present similar difficulties.

As a further aid to the students, two appendices are provided. One covers words with affirmative and negative distribution, the other words with count and mass noun distribution. These two patterns especially are the source of much confusion among students of English (and indeed, among native speakers as well).

This book is offered in the hope that it will help students of English to overcome their difficulties with some common words that create uncommon problems for them in mastering their new language.

a

a/an

1. **A** and **an** are the indefinite articles. They are used with singular count nouns *(chair, flower, desk)* that are previously unidentified or unspecified.

   We need *a chair* in this room.
   I'd like to get *a new desk*.

2. When the reference to a noun is specific, the definite article *the* is used.

   We need *a chair* in this room; *the chair* in your bedroom would look good here.
   I'd like to get *a new desk; the desk* that I have now is falling apart.

3. **A** is used before a consonant sound; **an** is used before a vowel sound.

   I haven't been to *a movie* for *a long time*.
   He wanted to be *an actor*, but he ended up as *an attendant* at *a gas station*.

4. **A** and **an** are also used as prepositions to mean "in each of a unit of measurement such as time, weight, and so on."

   These apples cost ninety-five cents *a pound*.
   A plumber can earn twenty dollars *an hour* or more.

   Per is sometimes used in the same sense, but **a** and **an** are much more frequent.

   Plumbers can make a lot of money *per hour*.

about

1. **About** is a preposition with several different meanings. It indicates the subject of talking, thinking, and so on.

5

Debbie talks *about her plans*, but she never carries them out.

I can't help thinking *about all the good times we've had*.

Of is sometimes used in the same sense.

Karen talks *of her ideas* as though they were completely new.

I'm thinking *of taking a vacation* in July.

2. **About** also indicates something connected with or related to.

I want to get more information *about computers*.

3. **About** also indicates motion in an indefinite or uncertain direction, or the presence of someone or something at an indefinite place.

He always walks *about his office* while he's talking on the phone.

She left her keys somewhere *about the house*, but she can't find them now.

4. With quantities or numbers, **about** is used as an adverb to mean "approximately, more or less."

She reads *about a hundred books* a year, maybe a few more, maybe a few less.

It's *about four o'clock*, give or take a couple of minutes.

I bought *about a pound of strawberries*, maybe an ounce more, maybe an ounce less.

5. **How about?** and **What about?** are used to ask questions about something that is more or less coincidental to the conversation.

"We don't need gas." "That's good, but *how about oil?*"

"I haven't heard from my brother for a long time." *"What about your sister?* Have you heard from her recently?"

6. **About to,** followed by the basic form of the verb, is used to indicate an action that will take place in the immediate future.

> Hurry! The train's just *about to leave.*
>
> Kevin was *about to go out* when the phone rang.
>
> Come on, finish dinner. Your favorite TV program is *about to begin.*

ago

Ago is used with time expressions to refer to an action completed in the past. It is unusual because it follows the time expression rather than coming before it.

> I lived in that house *four years ago,* but I haven't seen it since then.
>
> You should have started making plans for your vacation *a week ago.*
>
> Jennifer bought a new car *a month ago.*

all

1. **All** indicates the entire number or amount of the noun that follows. It is used with plural count nouns and mass nouns.

> She's read *all the books* in the house.
>
> I've paid *all the bills* that were due.
>
> They had already loaded *all the baggage* on the airplane.
>
> I have *all the information* I need.

2. **All** considers an entire number or amount as a whole, whereas **every** considers the things or persons in a group separately, one by one. **Every** is used with singular count nouns.

> She's read *all the books* in the house.
> She's read *every book* in the house.
> I've paid *all the bills* that were due.
> I've paid *every bill* that was due.

7

3. In one special sense, meaning "wholly, entirely, completely," **all** can be used with singular count nouns.

> It's really very kind of you to help me with my errands. I always tell everybody that you're *all heart*.
>
> Everything about Janice is very dainty, very feminine. She's *all woman*.

almost

1. **Almost** means "nearly, not quite, just short of."

> It's *almost three miles* from my house to the station; to be exact, it's two and nine-tenths miles.
>
> The plane was *almost on time;* it was only five minutes late.
>
> Jessica's *almost ready;* she'll be with you in ten minutes or so.

2. Note that **about** can mean "more or less," but **almost** always means "a little less."

> It was *about five* when we left the office. (It could have been a few minutes before or a few minutes after.)
>
> It was *almost five* when we left the office. (It was a few minutes before.)

already

1. **Already** means "before a definite or implied time." It can occur before a main simple verb or after the first auxiliary in a verb phrase; it can also occur at the end of the sentence.

> *I've already read* this book.
> *I've read* this book *already*..
>
> She *already answered* that question.
> She *answered* that question *already*.

2. **Already** is used in affirmative statements or in affirmative and negative questions; **yet** is used in negative statements or in affirmative or negative questions.

I've *already bought* my ticket.
He *hasn't bought* his ticket *yet*.

Have you *checked* the oil *already?*
Have you *checked* the oil *yet?*

Haven't you *already checked* the oil?
Haven't you *checked* the oil *yet?*

3. **Already** shouldn't be confused with **all ready,** which means "completely ready."

We'll have these letters *all ready* in a few minutes; then you can take them to the post office.

We're *all ready* to leave on our vacation; our bags are packed, the car is waiting; we don't need to do anything more.

also

1. **Also** means "in addition."

I'm going to study math next year, and I'm *also* going to take a course in physics. (In addition to math, I'm going to study physics next year.)

2. **Too** is also frequently used with the same meaning as **also.** In this sense, **too** usually comes at the end of the sentence, whereas **also** usually occurs before a simple main verb *(runs, walked)* or after the first auxiliary verb in a verb phrase.

Donna uses a computer at work; she *also has* one at home.
Donna uses a computer at work, and she *has* one at home *too.*

I've read all the letters, and I've *also answered* them.
I've read all the letters, and I've *answered* them *too.*

3. Both **also** and **too** are used in affirmative statements and affirmative and negative questions, whereas **either** is used in negative statements and negative questions.

Donna doesn't use a computer at work, and she doesn't have one at home *either.*

9

Have they *also* eaten the oranges?

Have they eaten the oranges *too?*

Haven't they eaten the oranges *either?*

another

1. **Another** means "one more" or "one different."

   We can't get *another person* in this room; it's so crowded now that we can't cram one more in here.

   You didn't like that pair of shoes? Here, I have *another pair* to show you. It's a different style, so you may like it better.

2. **Another** can be used as an adjective, as in the examples above, or as a pronoun.

   That apple was delicious. Do you have *another* that I can take home with me?

   I didn't like this book at all. Do you have *another* that you think I might enjoy more?

any

1. **Any** is used with plural count nouns *(books, apples, shoes)* or mass nouns *(paper, water, information)*. **Any** has a function similar to the indefinite articles **a** and **an** in introducing a previously unidentified or unspecified noun.

   There aren't *any stamps* on your desk.

   Didn't she buy *any apples?*

   Are there *any good programs* on TV tonight?

   Vanessa didn't write down your address; she couldn't find *any paper*.

   There wasn't *any water* in the pool so we couldn't go swimming.

   We don't have *any information* about the new tax law yet.

2. **Any** is used in negative statements or in affirmative or negative questions in this use, whereas **some** is used in affirmative statements or affirmative or negative questions.

10

We have *some new typists* in the office.
We don't have *any new typists* in the office.

Do we have *some new typists* in the office?
Do we have *any new typists* in the office?

Don't we have *some new typists* in the office?
Don't we have *any new typists* in the office?

3. **Any** is also used as a pronoun in negative statements and affirmative and negative questions with the same general meaning of an indefinite number or amount.

"Why didn't you buy *any fruit?*" "There wasn't *any* that was good enough."

"Did you get *any paper?*" "We don't need *any.*"

"Will you get *some chairs?*" "There aren't *any* in here."

4. **Any** is frequently used to mean "no matter which or whom of more than two." Note that in this meaning, **any** can be used with singular count nouns. It can also be used in affirmative statements in this meaning.

I'll be able to visit you *any day* next week that's all right with you.

That child eats *any food* you put in front of him.

Any information you can get about the new regulation will be helpful.

Any job you get will be better than none.

anybody/anyone/anything

1. These words are among the group known as indefinite pronouns, which refer to unspecified persons or objects or to persons and objects in general. **Anybody** and **anyone** refer to persons and are interchangeable; **anything** refers to objects. They have the same affirmative and negative distribution with the **some-** words as **any** does with **some**.

I want *somebody* to help me.
I don't want *anybody* to help me.

You've done *something* wrong.
You haven't done *anything* wrong.

11

2. In contrast to the usual practice in English, adjectives come after rather than before the indefinite pronouns.

> It's such a hot day! Don't you have *anything cold* to drink?
>
> I didn't meet *anyone interesting* at all at the party.

3. All three of these **any-** words can be used like **any** to express the idea of "no matter who, no matter what."

> You can do this job. I'm sure you can; *anyone* can do it with a little training.
>
> *Anything* you decide will be all right with me; it really doesn't matter to me.

anyhow/anyway/any which way

1. Both **anyhow** and **anyway** mean "in any manner or way, in any event."

> We might as well leave now; we can't finish this job tonight *anyhow*, no matter how hard we try.

2. **Anyhow** is the negative member of an affirmative-negative pair with **somehow**.

> You'll be able to answer all the questions *somehow*.
>
> You won't be able to answer all the questions *anyhow*.

3. **Anyhow** is sometimes used to mean "carelessly." The phrase **any which way** expresses the same idea.

> Janice just filed the correspondence *anyhow;* she didn't even try to alphabetize it.
>
> David just throws his clothes around *any which way* at all; he expects somebody to come along and pick up after him.

4. Both **anyhow** and **anyway,** but especially **anyway,** often act as sentence connectors.

> It's too early to go to bed; *anyway*, there's a program on TV that I want to watch.

1. **Any more** is part of an affirmative-negative pair with **still** when **still** is used to indicate an action that continues or continued up to a certain time. **Still** is used in affirmative statements and **any more** is used in negative statements.

   Jennifer's *still* studying computer languages.
   Jessica isn't studying computer languages *any more*.

   Carol *still* kept on dieting even after she'd lost five pounds.
   Helen didn't keep on dieting *any more* after she'd lost five pounds.

   Note that **still** occurs before a simple main verb or after the first auxiliary in a verb phrase, whereas **any more** occurs at the end of a sentence or a clause.

2. In contrast to most affirmative-negative pairs, **any more** does not usually occur in affirmative questions but only in negative questions.

   Does Mark *still* exercise every morning?
   Doesn't he exercise every morning *any more?*

   Is she *still* dieting?
   Isn't she dieting *any more?*

3. Occasionally, **any more** is also used in negative sentences to mean "now or nowadays," referring to the general present rather than the present moment.

   You can't find many inexpensive restaurants *now*.
   You can't find many inexpensive restaurants *any more*.

   Forty seems young to me *nowadays*.
   Forty doesn't seem young to me *any more*.

anyplace/anywhere

1. **Anyplace** and **anywhere**, like the **any-** words, are affirmatively and negatively distributed with the corresponding **some-** words.

   She's found *somewhere* to live.

   She hasn't found *anywhere* to live.

2. Both **anyplace** and **anywhere** are used in affirmative statements with the meaning of "no matter where."

> *Anywhere* you want to go is all right with me; it doesn't matter where.
>
> There were always a lot of people around *anyplace* they went.

3. **Anyplace** is sometimes written as two words, but modern usage favors the one-word form.

as

1. **As** is used as a conjunction with meaning "the way that, the manner that."

> I'll prepare this fish just *as* you like it.
>
> Nothing ever turns out *as* I expect it to.

2. Many people use **like** as a conjunction in the same sense, but this is considered non-standard even though it occurs widely among native speakers of English.

3. **As . . . as** is used with adjectives and adverbs in so-called comparisons of equality, that is, to express the idea of "to the same degree or extent."

> Jim's *as tall as* his brother even though he's more than a year younger.
>
> The car won't get you into town *as fast as* the train.
>
> We've had *as much rain* this week *as all last month*.
>
> Paul doesn't always take care of his car *as carefully as* he should.

4. When **as** is used in comparisons of equality, it is a conjunction, not a preposition, and therefore should be followed by a subject personal pronoun.

> She's not *as old as I* (am).
>
> He didn't eat *as much as she* (did).

5. **The same . . . as** is used with nouns for comparisons of equality.

> I wear *the same size shirt as* you do.
>
> They always go to *the same restaurant as* we do every Saturday night.

6. **As** follows **the same** directly when **the same** is used as a pronoun.

> My hometown is *the same as* hers.

7. **As if** and **as though** are used to introduce clauses and mean "the way it would be if."

> Luke acts *as if he was the boss.* (He isn't the boss, but he acts that way.)
>
> It was January, but the day was so warm that it felt *as though it were spring already.*

Note the use of *were* instead of *was* in the second sentence; this use emphasizes the feeling that the statement in the clause is not true, that it is contrary to fact.

8. **As** is used as a conjunction in time clauses with the meaning "at the same time as."

> The plane was landing *just as we got to the airport.*
>
> The telephone rang *as I was walking into the house.*

9. **As** is also occasionally used like **because** or **since** to introduce clauses of reason.

> He won't buy a word processor *as he thinks it won't do him any good.*
>
> She had to walk to work *as the bus drivers were out on strike.*

10. **As** is used as a preposition with the meaning of "in the capacity of, with the function of."

He loves to play football; *as captain,* he has led his team to several victories.

You should use "like" *as a preposition* and "as" *as a conjunction.*

As a singer Marcy's superb, but *as an actress* she's not at her best.

11. **As for** and **as to** are both used as prepositions with the meaning of "concerning, regarding, in reference to."

    I look at magazines, but *as for books,* I just never have time to read them.

    I'll take the magazines with me. *As to the books,* I'd like to have them sent; they're too heavy to carry.

12. **As such** means "by or of itself."

    Your resumé as such isn't as important as the impression you make in the interview.

    Her looks as such aren't all that wonderful, but she has so much vivacity that everyone thinks she's attractive.

    For more examples of **as such,** see the entry for *such.*

13. **Such as** means "for example, for instance, similar to."

    Fred's taking a lot of math courses *such as trigonometry and calculus.*

    There are many sources of information, *such as newspapers, radio, and television,* in the world today.

    See the entry for **such** for more examples of *such as.*

14. **As well,** used as an adverb, and **as well as,** used as a preposition, are expressions that indicate the idea of "in addition" or "in addition to."

    I'll take that jacket, and I'*d like to take this shirt as well.*

    I studied one year of Greek *as well as four years of Latin.*

16

Don't confuse **as well as** meaning "in addition to" with **as well as** in a comparison of equality for the adverb or adjective **well,** as in the example below.

The old woman complained that she *couldn't hear as well as she used to.*

15. **As is** is a colloquial expression that is used to indicate that something is acceptable without any changes.

I can wear that jacket *as is;* it won't need any alterations at all.

16. **As yet** means "up till now."

I haven't heard from her *as yet,* but I expect to get a letter soon.
It's nine o'clock. She hasn't finished her homework *as yet,* but she should be finished by nine-thirty or ten.

17. **As of** means "by a particular time."

He'll be twenty-one years old *as of the tenth of November.*
As of the end of May she'll have finished all her required courses.

18. **As** can be used in shortened sentences with the meaning "and also." It is a somewhat formal substitute or alternate for *and so.*

Helen and Tom work in an office, *and I work in an office also.*
Helen and Tom work in an office, *and so do I.*
Helen and Tom work in an office, *as do I.*

Note that an auxiliary verb follows **as.** With the present tense, the auxiliary is *do* or *does;* with the past tense, *did;* and with verb phrases, the first auxiliary with which the phrase is formed.

I *took* the day off, *as did* my friend.

She'*ll be attending* the university next year, *as will* her brother.

19. **So as** followed by an infinitive indicates purpose. It is an equivalent of **in order to.**

> We left very early, at five o'clock in the morning. *so as to avoid* the heavy traffic.
>
> We left early *in order to avoid* the heavy traffic.

See the entry for **so** for more examples of **so as** plus an infinitive.

ask

1. **Ask** is used chiefly in two senses: to ask a question or to request something, in which case it is followed by **for.**

> "Why didn't you call me last night?" I *asked.*
>
> She *asked* where I was going.
>
> I *asked* her whether I could see her again.
>
> I *asked Claire for her phone number*, but she wouldn't give it to me.
>
> She *asked for spinach* but got broccoli instead.

2. **Ask** is sometimes used to mean "invite."

> They *asked us* to their party Saturday night. Have they invited you too?

3. **Ask** is also used to introduce indirect quotations of requests, that is, polite imperatives.

> Please don't walk on the grass.
> They *asked* us not to walk on the grass.
>
> Will you please get me a glass of water?
> She *asked* me to get her a glass of water.

4. In indirect quotations of the imperative, **ask** contrasts with **tell.** As noted, *ask* is used with requests or polite imperatives, whereas *tell* is used with orders or commands.

18

"Please take off your shirt," the doctor said.
The doctor *asked* me to take off my shirt.

"Take one of these pills first thing in the morning," the doctor said.
The doctor *told* me to take one of these pills first thing in the morning.

"Please check these figures for me," she said.
She *asked* me to check these figures for her.

"Send the package by special delivery," I said.
I *told* him to send the package by special delivery.

at

1. **At** is a very common preposition with a wide variety of uses in expressions of place, time, and manner. **At** is often confused by students of English with two other very common prepositions, **in** and **on**. In place expressions, **at** denotes near, almost touching; **in** denotes inside, within some kind of definite limits; and **on** denotes on top of, on the surface of.

   We were sitting *at our desks*.
   The desks were *in the classroom*.
   Our books were *on our desks*.

   We ate lunch *at a cafeteria*.
   The cafeteria is *in our office building*.
   There's a sign *on the cafeteria door* that says Employees Only.

2. **At** is used for specific places and often has a very strong sense of purpose. **In,** on the other hand, merely indicates the presence of something or someone in an enclosed space.

   She was *at the bank* when I saw her; she was cashing a check.
   I saw a lot of people *in the bank*, so I didn't bother to enter.

   I saw her *at the office*, but she was so busy I didn't get a chance to talk to her.
   I often see her *in the office*.

   He had to stay *in the hospital* several days. (He was a patient.)

19

I met her *at the hospital* when she was visiting her brother.
The doctor has to spend several hours *at the hospital* every day. (She works *at the hospital.*)

Note that with *hospital,* **in** denotes being a patient, whereas **at** denotes either a short visit or employment there.

She's just started her freshman year, so she'll be *in school* for four more years.
I was *at school* yesterday morning to register for my courses next semester.

Note that **in school** denotes being a student for a long period of time, while **at school** denotes being there at a particular time or with the purposes of attending classes.

3. **At** is used with a complete address, one that includes the house or building number, whereas **on** is used when only the street is given.

   The store is *at 900 Fifth Avenue.*
   The store is *on Fifth Avenue.*
   He lives *at 96 State Street.*
   He lives *on State Street.*

4. **At** is used in a number of common place expressions.

   I'm always *at home* in the evening.
   We're *at dinner* now; please call later.
   They usually discuss business *at lunch.*
   We can't make personal phone calls *at work.*

5. In time expressions, **at** is used for specific times; that is, with the hours of the day.

   Your flight to New York will leave *at 10:15.*
   I get up *at six o'clock* every morning.
   I'll meet you at the theater *at eight* this evening.

20

6. **On** is used in time expressions with days of the week, days of the month, and with the names of holidays.

>I had dinner with my friends *on Friday*.
>
>I have an appointment with the dentist *on the 23rd of June*.
>
>She started working here *on March 28*.
>
>The summer season ends *on Labor Day*.
>
>We always have dinner with the whole family *on Thanksgiving*.

However, when an entire holiday season – Christmastime rather than just Christmas Day — is meant, **at** is used.

>We'll fly home *at Thanksgiving* and stay the whole weekend.
>
>We always have a few days' vacation *at Easter*.

7. **In** is used with the larger divisions of time —months, seasons, years, and centuries.

>We'll start school again *in September*.
>
>I'm going to take a short vacation *in February*.
>
>It gets very hot here *in the summer*.
>
>All the flowers that I plant *in the fall* will bloom *in the spring*.
>
>He came to this country *in 1985*.
>
>She graduated from the university *in 1980*.
>
>The United States became independent *in the eighteenth century*.
>
>They're writing a composition about what they think life will be like *in the twenty-first century*.

8. **At** is also used in several other common time expressions.

>I always have lunch *at noon*.
>
>The children are tired because they stayed up late; they went to bed *at midnight*.
>
>He'd rather work *at night;* he likes to sleep during the day.

21

Linda and I usually get to work *at the same time* in the morning.

I always get up *at dawn;* the light wakes me up.

They like to sit outdoors *at sunset* and watch the changing colors in the sky.

9. See the entries for **in** and **on** for more examples of their uses in place and time expressions.

10. **At** is used with verbs of motion or with verbs like *smile, laugh, shout,* and so on, in the sense of "toward, in the direction of."

   I don't know that man who's *waving at me.*

   All the other students *laughed at me* when I made a mistake.

   You don't need to *shout at me;* I can hear you perfectly well.

   With *throw,* **at** indicates the intention of hitting someone or something, whereas **to** indicates that the intention is for someone to catch the object thrown.

   He got mad and *threw the ball at me*, but he didn't hit me.

   I told them not to *throw stones at the dog.*

   You stand over there and I'll *throw the ball to you;* then when you catch it, you can *throw it back to me.*

11. **At** is also used in several common expressions of manner, expressions that show the way in which something is done or that denote a state or condition.

   I'm never *at ease* during a job interview.

   The officer made the soldiers stand *at attention.*

   We're not *at liberty* to take those books out of the library.

   The soldiers were *at rest*, but they snapped to attention when the general walked in.

   She felt strange in her new job for a while, but she's completely *at home* with it now.

Note that **at home** in the last sentence is not a place expression but has a meaning similar to **at ease.**

12. **At** is also used with ages, speeds, levels, and so on.

> *At the age of 40,* he felt that he hadn't gotten very far with his career.
> The plane cruises *at about 500 miles an hour.*
> The plane was cruising *at 30,000 feet.*
> These shirts were a bargain; they were on sale *at $12.95.*

at all

At all follows a negative (or negatively distributed expressions like the **any-** words) and serves to make the negative more emphatic. It can occur directly after the negative or at the end of a negative sentence or clause.

> Are you cold? No, not *at all.*
> I don't seem to be making *any progress at all* with this work.
> The children don't have *anything at all* to do.
> We've had hardly *any rain at all* this summer.

b

barely   see the entry for *hardly*

beside/besides

1. **Beside** is a preposition that means "next to" in its most common use.

> I sit *beside a window* in the office.
> My house is right *beside the town park.*

23

2. **Besides** is a preposition that means "in addition to" or an adverb that means "in addition."

Besides a new television set, we're going to get a VCR. (We're going to get a VCR in addition to a new television set.)

I'm not going to the party. I'm very tired. *Besides,* I don't have anything to wear.

a bit (of)

1. **A bit of** means "a small amount or quantity of." It is similar in meaning to **a little,** and like **a little,** it is followed by a mass noun.

   It will take quite *a bit of work* before the house is ready to move in.

   Wait for me a second. I have *a bit of sand* in my shoe; I'm having trouble walking.

2. **A bit** can be followed directly by an infinitive or used alone as a pronoun, replacing a noun or with the noun understood.

   I'm not hungry now. I had *a bit to eat* a little while ago.

   My mother put *a lot of food* on the table, but I could only eat *a bit.*

3. **A bit** also means "a short period of time."

   Let me think about that *a bit.* I'll have the answer for you in a minute or two.

4. **A bit of** also has the meaning "a piece of." It is one of the many expressions in English to indicate the countable particles of mass nouns, like *a drop of rain, a grain of sand,* and so on.

   Matthew had several *bits of string* in his pocket.

   They gave me little *bits of information,* but I couldn't get the whole story out of them.

24

5. **A bit** is also used as an intensifier with *more, less,* and the comparative degree of adjectives.

> I felt very sick yesterday, but I feel *a bit better* today.
>
> Vanessa drinks quite *a bit more coffee* than she should.
>
> John has *a bit less experience* than we want for that job.

Note that the nouns after *more* and *less* are mass nouns.

6. **A bit** is also used like **at all** as an emphatic after *not.*

> Was he sorry that he broke the window? No, *not a bit.*

borrow/lend

Borrow and **lend** cause confusion for many students of English because some languages have only one verb for the two English verbs. **Borrow** means "to receive a loan, to take money or something else from another person on a temporary basis." **Lend** means "to make or give a loan," that is, "to give money or something else on a temporary basis."

> I *borrowed* some money from my cousin. (I received some money from my cousin, but I'll have to pay him back.)

> My cousin didn't want to *lend* me the money, but he did anyway. (My cousin didn't want to give me the money; he only did it because I told him I'd pay him back next week.)

C

a couple of

1. **Couple** refers to two objects or people that are joined together.

> Mr. and Mrs. Johnson are a very happy *couple.*

2. **A couple of,** however, is much less exact. It may refer to any small unspecified number.

25

I'll be ready in *a couple of minutes;* it shouldn't be more than five minutes at the most.

She still has *a couple of letters* to answer, maybe two, maybe three, but not too many.

d

Demonstratives

1. The demonstratives are **this/these** and **that/those.** They are used both as adjectives and pronouns. As their name indicates, they point out someone or something in time or space in relation to the speaker. **This** and **these** refer to something near the speaker, while **that** and **those** refer to something farther away or more remote.

   This is my book right here on my desk; *that's yours* over there on the windowsill.

   These records are new; *those records* are the ones I bought last year.

2. **These** is the plural form of **this,** and **those** is the plural form of **that.**

   This record that I'm playing now is new.
   These records that I'm playing now are new.

   I threw away *that record* that I bought last year.
   I threw away *those records* that I bought last year.

3. The demonstratives are the ONLY adjectives in English that have singular and plural forms; otherwise, English adjectives do not change form.

   This old shirt doesn't fit me any more.
   These old shirts don't fit me any more.

   I can still wear *that old shirt.*
   I can still wear *those old shirts.*

do/make

1. Many students of English confuse the verbs **do** and **make,** since some languages have only one verb that corresponds to the two English verbs. The basic meaning of **do** is "to perform an action," whereas the basic meaning of **make** is "to create."

   She always *does* her work carefully. (She performs the action of working carefully.)
   She *makes* a lot of work for everybody else. (She creates work for other people to do.)
   Bill's always *doing* something; he likes to keep busy all the time. (He's always performing some kind of action or another.)
   Tanya likes to *make* things; she's tried painting and knitting and sewing at one time or another. (She likes to create things.)

2. The two words are combined in the colloquial expression **make do,** which means "to get along with what is available."

   I didn't go to the grocery store today, so we'll have to *make do* for dinner with what I can find in the refrigerator.

3. The two words are also contrasted in the expressions **do good,** "to perform a generous or beneficial action," and **make good,** "to become successful."

   Bob's always trying to *do good* by helping his friends with money or advice.

   It's difficult to *make good* as an actress, but she says she's going to keep on trying.

4. **Do** is also one of the most common auxiliary verbs in English. It is used for forming questions and negatives in the simple present and past tenses.

   They *work* in an office.
   Do they *work* in an office?
   They *don't work* in an office.

27

He *walks* to work.
Does he *walk* to work?
He *doesn't walk* to work.

She *got* her degree last year.
Did she *get* her degree last year?
She *didn't get* her degree last year.

5. **Do** is also used as an auxiliary in the simple present and past tenses to emphasize the verb. In this case, the form of **do,** NOT the main verb, is stressed.

   She <u>*does*</u> like her job.

   I <u>*did*</u> eat all my vegetables.

6. **Do** is also used in a number of common expressions. **Do away with** means "to get rid of, to eliminate."

   We'll *do away with* a lot of this paperwork when we get a computer.

7. **Do a favor** means "to perform a kind or generous action." You can do someone a favor or do a favor **for** someone.

   He *did me a big favor* by lending me twenty dollars last week.

   He won't *do a favor for anyone;* he won't even tell anyone what time it is.

8. **Do over** means "to repeat an action again."

   You'll have to *do over* this report; the boss didn't like it, and he wants some changes in it.

   I hate to *do things over;* I like to get them right the first time.

9. **Do without** means "to get along without."

   When I saw the prices of cars this year, I decided I'd have to *do without* one for another year.

   She forgot to get milk when she went to the store, so we'll just have to *do without* this evening.

10. For additional uses of **make,** see the entry for **make.**

e

each

1. **Each,** like **all,** refers to an entire group or class of people or things. **Each,** however, considers the individual person or thing in the group separately, one by one. Whereas **all** is used with mass nouns or plural count nouns, **each** is used with singular count nouns.

   All the records in the store are on sale.
   Each record in the store is on sale.

   She's read *all the books* in the house.
   She's read *each book* in the house with great care.

2. To emphasize the singularity of **each,** it is frequently followed by **one** and a phrase beginning with **of** to indicate the group or class.

   Each one of these records is on sale.
   Each one of the apartments in this building has a view of the river.

   Note that **each one** is followed by a singular verb form.

3. **Each** and **every** have the same general meaning, and they both follow the same grammatical pattern. **Each,** however, emphasizes the idea of singularity or individuality to a greater degree than **every.** In fact, the phrase **each and every** is sometimes used to give special emphasis.

   I get up at six o'clock in the morning *each and every day* of my life.

either

1. **Either** is part of an affirmative-negative pair with **also** or **too. Also** and **too** are used in affirmative statements and questions, whereas **either** is used in negative statements and questions.

29

She's going to visit her parents in San Francisco. She's *also* going to stop in Los Angeles.

She isn't going to visit her parents in San Francisco. She isn't going to stop in Los Angeles *either*.

Bill has some time to rest. Do you have some *too?*

Bill doesn't have any time to rest. Don't you have any *either?*

Note that **either** normally comes at the end of a sentence or a clause.

2. **Either** is used in shortened sentences in the same sense.

My friends didn't go to the beach last weekend, and I didn't *either*.

Helen couldn't answer the question, and I couldn't *either*.

3. Such shortened sentences are sometimes shortened still further to the colloquial expression **Me either.**

"I don't want to go home now." *"Me either."*

Do NOT, however, use **neither** as a substitute for **either** in this colloquial expression. The negative is understood with **either**, while **neither** makes a double negative, which is nonstandard usage.

4. **Or** is a conjunction that indicates an alternate or a choice. **Either** is often used with **or** to emphasize the alternate or choice. **Either** then precedes the first of the choices.

She's going to buy *either a VCR or a cassette player* next month.

Either his wife or his mother makes lunch for him every day.

Note that a singular verb form follows **either . . . or** when both the nouns are singular.

5. **Either** sometimes occurs alone as a pronoun when the alternate choices have already been given.

She's going to study *chemistry or physics* next semester. *Either* (that is, either chemistry or physics) will help her if she's going to study engineering.

else

1. **Else** is frequently used after the indefinite pronouns, the *some-*, *any-*, and *no-* pronouns, or with the related adverbs like *somewhere, anywhere,* and so on. **Else** indicates something or someone different or more.

   Can't *anyone else* solve this problem? It isn't really that difficult.

   Everyone else in my crowd went out last night, but I stayed home.

   You'll have to sit *somewhere else;* this seat is reserved.

2. **Else** also follows the question words *(where, who, what,* and so on) with the same general meaning as with the indefinite pronouns.

   What else can we do tonight? We've already done everything I can think of.

   Who else wants to go on the picnic? We have enough food for several more people.

   Sarah's not feeling well. *Why else* do you think she'd miss the dance?

3. The phrase **or else** is used to introduce an alternative to, or a consequence of, a previous statement. It often has a warning or even a threatening significance.

   You must eat a balanced diet *or else* you won't be healthy.

   She'll have to learn how to use a word processor *or else* she won't get that job.

   Do what your boss tells you to do *or else* you'll get in trouble.

   Go to bed now *or else!*

enough

1. **Enough** has the general meaning of "sufficient" or "sufficiently." It is used with mass nouns or plural count nouns.

31

I failed the exam because I didn't have *enough time* to finish. I needed a couple of hours, but they gave us only one.

There weren't *enough chairs* in the room for everyone to sit down.

2. Occasionally, **enough** occurs after the nouns, but this is no longer a very common usage.

We had *work enough* for a dozen people, but there were only three of us on duty.

3. **Enough** occurs AFTER adjectives or adverbs.

The job was *easy enough*, but it wasn't very interesting.

You haven't washed the car *carefully enough;* you'll have to do it over again.

4. **Enough of** can be used with singular count nouns.

It was *enough of a storm* to do a lot of damage.

She had *enough of a struggle* to get where she is today.

In this usage, **enough** (without *of a*) can follow the noun.

It was *strugggle enough* for her to get where she is today.

This is not a very frequent use of **enough,** but it may be encountered in movies or on TV in the rather common challenge *You're not man enough*, and so on.

even

1. As an adjective, **even** has several related meanings that include "equal," "level," "fair," and "regular." An *even number*, for example, is one that can be divided by two; the opposite is an *odd number*.

It was a very *even tennis match*. Both of the players were equally good.

The *land* here *is very even*. There aren't any hills anywhere around.

We made an *even exchange*. Neither one of us got cheated.

32

2. **Even** is frequently used as an adverb. One of its meanings as an adverb is "however improbable." It often suggests something that is unexpected or beyond normal expectations.

> Our team is great this year. We *even won* the big game against the team that's always beaten us before.
>
> Jennifer can solve mathematical problems in her head. She can *even work out* the problems in algebra without using pencil and paper.
>
> Bruce likes to do all the work around the house. He *even does* all the plumbing and electrical wiring himself.

3. When used with a negative, **even** has the sense of "in any way whatsoever."

> I can't get started on my homework. I *can't even figure out* what we're supposed to do.
>
> He's not at all qualified for the job. He *can't even use* a word processor.
>
> Frank gives up too easily. He *won't even try* to work through his problems.

4. **Even** can also be used to emphasize the truth of a statement.

> Sandra was always kind, *even affectionate*, but I knew she didn't love me.
>
> He's always willing, *even anxious*, to please all his friends.

5. **Even** also intensifies both the comparative and the superlative.

> The movie was *even better* than I expected.
>
> When I told him to slow down, he began driving *even faster*.
>
> The candidate had *even fewer* votes than the polls had predicted.
>
> *Even the least* noise in the classroom upsets the teacher.

Even the best student in the class had trouble with the exam.

Even the softest chair in the room wasn't comfortable enough for her.

6. **Even** is used with both *now* and *then* to emphasize that an action is or was happening at that very time.

   Here we are stuck in a traffic jam, and *even now* the curtain is going up on the show.

   Jessica was always drawing pictures when she was still a child; *even then* she showed a great deal of talent.

7. When *as* is used as a conjunction to introduce a time clause, **even** can strengthen the idea that two actions are happening at the same time.

   We pulled into the airport parking lot *even as* the plane was arriving.

8. **Even** is used with *if* to strengthen a condition. **Even if** means "notwithstanding, in spite of the possibility that."

   We're going on a picnic tomorrow *even if* it rains.
   We'll be at the party *even if* we're a little late.
   You wouldn't have enjoyed the party *even if* you'd been there.

9. **Even though** is used in the same sense as **even if**. **Even though** is also an equivalent of **although** or **though** in introducing a clause that contrasts with a previous clause.

   I didn't get the job *even though* I thought I'd done well on the interview.

   The children are playing outdoors *even though* it's quite cold today.

10. **To get even** means "to get revenge."

   Walter insulted me but I'm going *to get even* with him no matter how.

   It's silly to waste your time trying *to get even* whenever someone says something bad about you.

34

11. **To break even** means "to make neither a profit nor a loss, neither to win nor to lose."

> They*'re breaking even* in their store. They haven't made any money, but they haven't lost any either.
>
> I spend about as much money as I make every month. I just about *break even*. I never have any extra money.

ever

1. **Ever** is used in both affirmative and negative questions with the meaning "at any time."

> Did you *ever get* all those letters answered?
>
> Haven't you *ever read* <u>Moby Dick?</u> I thought it was assigned in school; I was sure everybody had read it at one time or another.

2. **Ever** is also used with **not** in negative statements where it has the same meaning as "never, not at any time."

> I *won't ever* forget the wonderful vacation we had in Spain last year. (I'll never forget it.)
>
> I *don't ever* get to sleep before midnight. (I never get to sleep before midnight.)

-ever words

1. **Ever** combines with all the question words—*what, when, where,* and so on. These -**ever** words are used as conjunctions with the meaning "no matter what," "no matter when," and so on.

> I'll meet you *whenever* you want; it doesn't matter when or where. I just want to see you.

2. The -**ever** words are also used as question words. They serve as emphatic variations on the simple question words, often with a connotation of disbelief or indignation.

> *However* did you manage to finish all that work? I thought you wouldn't be able to get through it for at least a month.
>
> *Wherever* have you been? I've been looking for you everywhere.

35

3. The colloquial expression **on earth** can follow the simple question words with the same connotation of disbelief or indignation as the **-ever** words.

> *Where on earth* did you get that hat? It looks terrible on you!
> *How on earth* am I going to finish all this work? It will take me a month to get through it all.

4. In addition to the above uses, **however** occurs as a sentence connector with the same significance as **but**; that is, it introduces a sentence or clause in opposition or contrast to a previous sentence or clause.

> We were supposed to play tennis this afternoon; *however*, it rained so we couldn't. (We were supposed to play tennis this afternoon, but it rained so we couldn't.)
> She expected to get a promotion this year. *However*, they passed her over, so now she's looking for another job.

every

1. **Every,** like **all,** refers to an entire group or class of people or things. **Every,** however, considers the individual thing or person in the group separately, one by one. Whereas **all** is used with mass nouns or plural count nouns, **every** is used with singular count nouns.

> *All the plans* I made came to nothing.
> *Every plan* I made came to nothing.
> We won *all our football games* last year.
> We won *every football game* we played last year.

2. **Every other** means "every second or alternate person or thing."

> I have to take one of these pills *every other day*. This is Monday, so I'm taking one today, and I'll take another on Wednesday, then on Friday, and so on.
> We get paid *every other week*. We got paid last week, so we won't get paid this week; we have to wait until next week.

3. The phrases **every now and then** and **every once in a while** mean "occasionally."

> I see a movie *every now and then*. I saw one last month, and I'll probably see another next month.
>
> The teacher likes to give us a surprise quiz *every once in a while*.

everybody/everyone/everything

1. These words are among those that are classified as indefinite pronouns because they refer to unspecified people or things or to people or things in general. **Everybody** and **everyone** refer to people and are interchangeable.

> *Everybody* I know has a car.
> *Everyone* I know has a car.
>
> *Everybody* is going to have a good time at the party.
> *Everyone* is going to have a good time at the party.

2. **Everything** refers to things or objects.

> *Everything* is ready for the party; all the food, the decorations, the music, *everything*'s done.

3. These words are singular, and they are followed by singular verb forms like *has* and *is* in the examples above. Pronouns that refer to these words should also be singular. Traditionally, **everyone** and **everybody** were followed by masculine singular pronouns unless it was clear from the context that the group was entirely feminine.

> *Everyone* on the plane had *his* seat belt fastened.
>
> *All the girls* in the class went on a trip to New York. They traveled by air. When the plane took off, *everyone* had *her* seat belt fastened.

Another acceptable form for the singular pronoun is *his or her*.

> *Everybody* on the plane had *his or her* seat belt fastened.
>
> *Everyone* in the class had *his or her* books closed during the test.

37

f

far/farther/farthest/further

1. **Far** means "distant in space or time." It is most often used in questions or in negative statements, whereas **a long way** is used in affirmative statements.

   Jack: How *far* is it to the next gasoline station?

   Fred: It isn't *far* now, only ten or twelve miles.

   Jack: That's *a long way* when we're almost out of gas.

   Jane: Do you live near your office?

   Mary: Oh, no! I live out in the suburbs. It's *a long way* from town. Luckily, my house isn't *far* from a subway station.

2. **Far** can be used directly before a noun in the sense of "distant in time or space."

   Are those mountains I see in the *far distance?*

   Who knows what the technology of the *far future* will be like?

3. The expression **so far** means "up to this point in time."

   I haven't gotten a job *so far*, but I'm still trying.

4. **As far as** and **so far as** mean "to the extent that."

   We haven't had any trouble with the new computer *as far as* I know, but there may be some developments they haven't told me about.

   I haven't broken any rules *so far as* I'm aware.

5. **Far, by far,** and **far and away** can all be used as intensifiers with the comparative and superlative degrees of adjectives and adverbs.

   She's *far taller* than I was at her age.

   He's *by far the tallest* boy in the class.

38

This is *far and away the most difficult* exam we've had *so far*.

She checks her work *far more carefully* than she needs to.

This is *by far the hottest* day of the year.

6. The comparative and superlative forms of **far** are irregular, **farther** and **(the) farthest**.

Carmen lives *farther* away from the office than I do.

The farthest Pedro's ever been from home is about a hundred miles.

7. **Further** is an alternate form for **farther**. In general, however, **farther** is used only when speaking of distance, whereas **further** is used in other contexts.

We can't *go any farther;* the road has been blocked by a flood.

I need *further information* before I can go ahead with this report.

a few/few/fewer/the fewest

1. **A few** means "a small number." It is used with plural count nouns.

She got *a few books* out of the library. I don't know exactly how many, maybe five or six.

We still have *a few days*, a week or so, before we go on vacation.

2. **Few,** on the other hand, means "not many," and thus has a negative significance. It is also used with plural count nouns.

There weren't many cars on the street yesterday because it was a holiday.
There were *few cars* on the street yesterday because it was a holiday.

She didn't find many books that she wanted to read.
She found *few books* that she wanted to read.

39

3. **Fewer** and **the fewest** are the comparative and superlative forms of **few**. They are used in negative or minus comparisons; that is, they are the opposites of *more* and *the most*. Like **few,** they are used with plural count nouns.

> There aren't as many holidays in winter as in summer.
> There are *fewer holidays* in winter than in summer.
>
> She got a raise because she made *the fewest mistakes* in her work.

4. **A few** can be used to modify *more*.

> We've seen *a few more movies* this month than last.

Do NOT use **a few** to modify *less;* **a few** should be followed by a plural count noun, whereas *less* should be followed by a mass noun, so the two do not go together. **A few fewer** is possible, but it is so awkward that it should be avoided.

for/since

1. The difference in time expressions between **for** and **since** often presents difficulties for students of English. **For** indicates a period of time, whereas **since** indicates the time that the action started.

> I waited for her *for more than an hour.*
> I've been waiting for her *since four o'clock.*
>
> He worked in a factory *for four years.*
> He had worked in the factory *since 1983.*
>
> She's been dating that guy *for two months.*
> She's been dating that guy *since September.*

Note that **since** is used with perfect verb phrases, those that are formed with the auxiliary *have.*

2. Both **for** and **since** are used as conjunctions with the same meaning as **because.**

> *Since* she had a lot of homework to do last night, she had to stay home.

People were astonished at his knowledge, *for* he had never had a formal education.

For in this sense is much more formal and literary than either **because** or **since.**

front/in front of

1. The **front** of something is the side that faces forward. The front of a building, for example, is the side that faces the street. The front of a classroom is the most important side of the room, usually the side where the teacher's desk is located. The front of an auditorium is the side nearest the stage.

   > Mary doesn't hear well, so she always wants to sit in the *front of the room,* as close to the teacher's desk as possible.

   > They have a small *front yard* (on the street side of the house) but a big back yard (behind the house, away from the street).

2. **In front of** is used in place expressions with the meaning of "before" or "ahead of."

   > I always wait for her *in front of the building* where she works (not across the street but at or near the *front entrance* of the building).

   > We were lucky. We found a parking space right *in front of the restaurant* where we were having dinner (not across the street but on the same side as the restaurant).

   > There were so many people *in front of me* (ahead of me) in the theater that I couldn't see anything.

3. **In front of** does NOT mean "across from" or "opposite."

   > The theater is opposite the hotel. (They are across the street from each other.)

   > There were so many cars *in front of my house* (on the same side of the street) that I had to park across the street.

further   see the entry for *far*

41

g

a good deal (of)   see the entry for ***a great deal (of)***

good for/good of

1. **Good for** indicates that the stated action will be beneficial to the object of the preposition **for**.

   Giving up smoking will be *good for you*. You'll feel a lot better.

   It will be *good for the company* to cut costs; they'll increase their profits if they do.

   It would be *good for her* to get more exercise; she'd be a lot healthier then.

2. **Good of** indicates approval of an action performed by the object of the preposition **of**.

   It was *good of you* to write that letter of recommendation for me. It helped me get the job.

   It was *good of her* to take care of the children for me. I was able to get out and do a lot of errands.

a great deal (of)

1. **A great deal of** means "a large amount or quantity of something." It is used with mass nouns.

   Daniel earns *a great deal of money*; it's more than enough for him to live on.

   A great deal of sand was washed away from the beach during the storm. Now we can't really use it any more.

2. **A good deal of** has the same meaning as **a great deal of**, but is generally understood to indicate not quite as large an amount as **a great deal of**.

   He earns *a good deal of money*, but he's often a little short of cash.

42

A good deal of sand was washed away from the beach during the storm, but there's enough left so we can still use the beach.

3. **A great deal of** can be used in affirmative and negative statements and questions. **Much,** however, which has the same meaning, is not often used after a verb in affirmative statements, and a **great deal of** is frequently used in its place.

Does Vanessa drink much coffee? Yes, she *drinks a great deal of coffee.*

I didn't have much experience, but she had *a great deal of* experience, so she got the job.

4. **A great deal** can be followed directly by an infinitive or used alone as a pronoun, replacing a noun or with the noun understood.

Don't bother me now. I have *a great deal to think about.*

Does she drink much coffee? Yes, *a great deal.*

5. Both **a great deal** and **a good deal** are used as intensifiers with *more, less,* and the comparative degree of adjectives and adverbs.

I need *a great deal more* information then I have now.

You eat *a good deal less* fruit than you should.

He's *a great deal better* at football than at basketball.

She's *a good deal happier* with her new job than with her old one.

Note that the nouns after *more* and *less* must be mass nouns.

h

hardly

1. When **hardly** is used in the sense of "almost not at all, not quite, not likely," it is a negative word. Therefore, it is used with the negatively distributed member of affirmative-

43

negative pairs, that is, with *any* instead of *some*, for example. Do NOT use a second negative such as *no* or *not* with **hardly**.

> I *hardly ever go* to the movies any more.
>
> I can *hardly hear anything* with that radio playing so loud.
>
> Simon can *hardly expect* to get a promotion yet; he's been here less than six months.

2. **Hardly** is the most common of a group of negative adverbs. Others in the group are **barely** and **scarcely**, with meanings very similar to **hardly**.

> We had a very bad connection; she could *barely hear anything* I said.
>
> Please hurry. We have *scarcely any time* to catch the plane.

her/hers see the entry for ***Possessive Forms***

his see the entry for ***Possessive Forms***

in

1. For a comparison of **in** and **at** in place expressions, see the entry for **at**. In addition to the uses given there, **in** is also used with the names of continents, nations, states, provinces, and cities. It is also used with the names of mountain ranges.

> China and India are both *in Asia*.
>
> I have friends *in India*.
>
> They live *in Bombay*.
>
> Canada is *in North America*.

Many people *in Canada* speak French.

Most of them live *in Quebec*, a province *in eastern Canada*.

I visited friends *in Montreal* last summer.

They spend the winter *in Florida* because it's much warmer than *in Minnesota*.

It's only September, but there's already been snow *in the Rockies*.

The highest mountains *in the world* are *in the Himalayas*.

2. **On,** however, is used with the names of islands when the word *island* (or *isle)* is included in the name. **On** is also used with the names of mountains when *mount* or *mountain* is used.

They've just bought a house *on Long Island*.

There's a big resort hotel *on Star Island*.

In spite of the danger, many people live *on Mount Vesuvius*.

The winds *on Mount Washington* are often violent.

3. There are several common place expressions with **in.**

I was *in bed* when the phone rang.

The executives always seem to be *in conference*.

She prefers living *in the city* to living *in the country*.

I left the library books *in the car*.

I found somebody's wallet *in the taxi*.

They like to spend the summer *in the mountains* where it's cool.

4. For a comparison of **in, at,** and **on** in time expressions, see the entry for **at. In** is also used in a number of common time expressions.

I always get up early *in the morning*.

I like to take a break sometime *in the afternoon*.

They usually watch television *in the evening*.

I'm frightened when I hear a strange sound *in the night*.

45

Note, however, that **at** is used with *night* when *the* is not included.

> There are a lot of strange sounds in the house *at night*.

Also, **on** is used with *morning, night, evening,* and so on, when the indefinite article *a* or *an* or some other indefinite expression comes before the time word.

> We had the accident *on a night* when there was a lot of ice on the road.
>
> We'll have our meeting *on some afternoon* next week, but I don't know yet which one.

On is also used with these time words when they are followed by an adjective clause or a prepositional phrase.

> I wasn't in the office *on the day when the computer was installed.*
>
> She didn't get to work on time *on the morning* of her birthday.

5. **In** is also used in several expressions of manner, expressions that indicate the way in which something is done or which denote a state or condition.

> Teachers often used to be paid *in kind* —with food or firewood or help with chores— rather than *in cash*.
>
> Her clothes are always *in fashion*.
>
> Make sure that what you say is *in order* before you speak up at the meeting.
>
> He always keeps his desk *in order;* nothing is ever out of place.
>
> That old mill hasn't been *in use* for many years.
>
> You'll have my report *in hand* by Monday morning at the latest.
>
> You should keep your statements to the press *in line* with government policy.

1. **It** is both a subject and object pronoun that refers to a noun that is neither masculine nor feminine.

   Helen: What's that thing you have there?
    Tom: *It's* a new kind of can opener.
   Helen: Oh, I don't want *it! It* looks too complicated. Put *it* away somewhere. I don't even want to see *it*.
    Tom: *It* could be very useful if you'd just try *it*.

2. **It** is used as the subject of sentences about the time of day.

   What time is *it* now? *It's* a quarter to ten.
   It's sunset; everything's growing dark.

3. **It** is used as the subject of sentences about the weather.

   It's raining now, but the weather report says *it'll* clear up this afternoon.

4. **It** is used as the subject of sentences with a number of impersonal adjectives such as *easy, difficult, possible, important, usual, customary,* and so on.

   It's easy to operate this machine. Here, let me show you how.
   It's important to check all the figures carefully.
   It's customary to take your hat off in the elevator.
   It's impossible for me to meet you before five o'clock.

its   see the entry for ***Possessive Forms***

j

just

1. **Just** is an adjective with the similar meanings of "fair," "unbiased," "deserving," "upright," and so on.

   Everyone thought the judge's decision was very *just;* she was able to punish the criminal and reward the victim.

   He tries to be *just* to all the students no matter whether he likes them personally or not.

2. Much more common is the use of **just** as an adverb with several different meanings. One of the meanings indicates a very short time before.

   The plane *just arrived;* the passengers haven't had time to pick up their baggage yet.

   We got to the theater *just before the curtain went up.*

3. **Just** can also mean "exactly" or "precisely."

   This sweater is *just what I wanted;* it's exactly what I was looking for.

4. Another meaning is "barely, narrowly."

   I *just missed the bus;* I was about a minute late.

5. **Just** can also be used to mean "only," in the sense of "no more than."

   There were *only a few seats* left in the theater.
   There were *just a few seats* left in the theater.

   They stayed *only a little while* because they had another appointment.
   They stayed *just a little while* because they had another appointment.

6. Colloquially, **just** is used as an intensifier with adjectives and adverbs. In this case, it has a meaning similar to **very** but usually shows a high degree of enthusiasm.

> The day is *just perfect* for a picnic! It's not too hot and there's not a cloud in the sky.

> The show was *just wonderful!* I've never enjoyed anything as much.

7. Another colloquial use of **just** is in the phrase **just about**, which means "almost."

> I'm *just about finished* with this letter; I'll be with you in five minutes.

> It was *just about midnight* before I got to bed last night.

k

kind of/sort of

1. Both **kind of** and **sort of** indicate that something or someone belongs to a type or class or group.

> She has exactly the *kind of experience* that we want for this job.
> She has exactly the *sort of experience* that we want for this job.
> I always feel gloomy on this *kind of day*, with all the clouds and rain.
> I always feel gloomy on this *sort of day*, with all the clouds and rain.
> She's the *kind of person* who succeeds in everything she tries.
> She's the *sort of person* who succeeds in everything she tries.

2. Both **kind of** and **sort of** are also used colloquially as intensifiers for adjectives and adverbs to mean "to a certain degree." In this use, they are similar in meaning to *rather* and *somewhat*.

49

She was *kind of angry* with me, but I was able to put her back in a good mood.

She was *sort of angry* with me, but I was able to put her back in a good mood.

The exam was *kind of difficult;* I don't know whether I passed it or not.

The exam was *sort of difficult;* I don't know whether I passed it or not.

l

the least   see the entry for *a little/little/less/the least*

lend   see the entry for *borrow/lend*

less   see the entry for *a little/little/less/the least*

like

1. **Like** is really two quite distinct words, a preposition and a verb, which are not related to each other. **Like,** the preposition, has the general meaning of "similar to, resembling, characteristic of."

   Tom enjoys all kinds of sports. He's just *like his father,* who was a great athlete.

   That chicken must have been very old; it tasted just *like rubber.*

   The setting sun was a brilliant red *like a great ball of fire.*

2. The use of **like** as a conjunction in place of **as, as if,** or **as though** has been increasing, even though it is considered nonstandard. The use of **like** as a conjunction should be avoided.

   You should take care of your VCR just *as* the instruction manual tells you.

50

It looks *as if* it's going to snow tonight.

While she was dancing, she felt *as though* the whole room were spinning around and around.

3. **Like,** the verb, means "to enjoy, to be pleasing to, to look on someone or something favorably."

I *like* to dance. (Dancing is pleasing to me.)

The boss *likes* the workers who always come in on time. (The boss looks favorably on those workers.)

She *doesn't like* her new job. (Her new job is not pleasing to her.)

My brother *likes* to work with his hands. (He enjoys working with his hands.)

You'*ll like* this book I'm reading. It's really great! (This book will be pleasing to you.)

She *didn't like* any of the paintings at the exhibition. (The paintings weren't pleasing to her.)

4. The common verb phrase **would like** is a polite equivalent of **want.**

Do you *want to go* dancing tonight?
Would you *like to go* dancing tonight?

She *wants to learn* at least one computer language.
She'*d like to learn* at least one computer language.

I *want to finish* these letters before I go out.
I'*d like to finish* these letters before I go out.

a little/little/less/the least

1. **A little** means "a small amount," and it is used with mass nouns.

She gets very upset if there's even *a little dust* in the house.

I try to drink *a little water* every day.

2. **A little** can be followed directly by an infinitive or used alone as a pronoun, replacing a noun or with the noun understood.

51

Please wait for me. I still have *a little to do* before I can leave, but I won't be too long.

"Do we have any bread at all?" "Just *a little*."

3. **Little** without the preceding *a*, on the other hand, means "not much" and thus has a negative significance. It is used with mass nouns.

There wasn't much food in the house, so I had to go to the store.
There was *little food* in the house, so I had to go to the store.
I couldn't get much information about the problem from my friends.
I could get *little information* about the problem from my friends.

4. **Less** and **the least** are the comparative and superlative forms of **little;** that is, they are the opposites of *more* and *the most*. Like **little,** they are used with mass nouns.

I didn't have as much experience as they wanted for the job.
I had *less experience* than they wanted for the job.
He didn't give us as much time as we needed to finish the job.
He gave us *less time* than we needed to finish the job.
You should plan to drive to New York on Saturday; you'll find that's the day with *the least traffic*.

5. **Less** and **the least** are also used in negative or minus comparisons with adjectives and adverbs.

This chair is *less comfortable than the couch*. (This chair isn't as comfortable as the couch.)
He was running *less quickly than I was*. (He wasn't running as quickly as I was.)
They made him sit in *the least comfortable chair in the room* while they fired questions at him.

6. **A little** is used as an intensifier with *more, less,* and the comparative degree of adjectives and adverbs.

52

We could use someone with *a little more experience* for that job.

We've had *a little less rain* than we need this year.

She was sick yesterday, but she feels *a little better* today.

You should take your job *a little more seriously*.

Note that the nouns after *more* and *less* are mass nouns.

7. Don't confuse the quantity words **a little** and **little** with the adjective **little,** which means "small" and is used with singular and plural count nouns.

   Bruce likes to buy a lot of *little* (small) *gadgets* for his kitchen.

   I've known him for years. I've known him since he was a *little child*.

a long way   see the entry for *far*

a lot (of)/lots (of)

1. Both **a lot of** and **lots of** mean "a large amount of" or "a large number of." There is no difference in meaning between the two expressions. They can be followed by either mass nouns or plural count nouns and can be used in all kinds of sentences—affirmative and negative statements and affirmative and negative questions. They are the most flexible expressions of quantity and number in English.

   Does he spend *a lot (lots) of money?*
   Doesn't he spend *a lot (lots) of money?*
   He spends *a lot (lots) of money.*
   He doesn't spend *a lot (lots) of money.*

   Does she have *a lot (lots) of friends?*
   Doesn't she have *a lot (lots) of friends?*
   She has *a lot (lots) of friends.*
   She doesn't have *a lot (lots) of friends.*

2. **Many** is sometimes used after a verb in affirmative statements; **a lot of** or **lots of,** however, are often substituted for **many.**

53

Does she *read a lot?*

She *reads a lot of books,* but she *doesn't read many magazines.*

3. **A lot** and **lots** can be followed directly by an infinitive or used alone as a pronoun, replacing a noun or with the noun understood.

   She's bought several compact discs, but she still has *a lot (lots) to get.*

   "Do you read many magazines?" "Yes, I do. I read *a lot.*"

4. Both **a lot** and **lots** can be used as intensifiers with *more, less, fewer,* and the comparative degree of adjectives and adverbs.

   There was *a lot more traffic* than I expected this morning.
   There was *lots more traffic* than I expected this morning.

   We've had *a lot less rain* than we need this summer.
   We've had *lots less rain* that we need this summer.

   She makes *a lot fewer mistakes* than anyone else in the office.
   She makes *lots fewer mistakes* than anyone else in the office.

   He was *a lot sicker* than he realized.
   He was *lots sicker* than he realized.

   His car was *a lot less expensive* than mine.
   His car was *lots less expensive* than mine.

m

make

1. For the difference in the basic meanings of **do** and **make,** see the entry for **do/make.**

2. **Make** is also frequently used in the sense of forcing someone to do something.

Sheila's glad they *made* her study math in school; it's been very useful in her job.

I always *make* the children help me with the housework; it teaches them good habits.

You just have to *make* yourself give up smoking; it takes will power.

3. **Make** is used in a large number of colloquial expressions. **Make out,** for example, is used in three different senses:

   a. To discern with difficulty:

   > The fog was so thick that I could just barely *make out* the car ahead of me.

   b. To write a check, a will, or so on:

   > You should *make out* the check to "cash," not to "bearer."

   c. To get along, to succeed:

   > She's had so much experience that she'll *make out* very well in her new job; everyone is sure she'll succeed in it.

4. **Make over** is used in two senses:

   a. To make again:

   > One of the seams was crooked, so she had to *make over* the whole dress.

   b. To assign:

   > When he decided to retire, he *made over* all his shares in the company to his children.

5. **Make** is combined with **up** in several different meanings, all of them quite common:

a. To become friends again after a quarrel:

> They had a fight several years ago, but they finally *made up* last week, and now they're friends again.

b. To put on cosmetics:

> Karen spent a lot of time *making up* her face before the interview; she wanted to look her very best.

c. To take a course or exam that one has missed:

> When I go to college, I'll have to *make up* some of the math courses I didn't take in high school.

d. To prepare:

> After every business trip, she has to *make up* a report on everything she did and learned.

e. To invent, to create:

> Nancy likes to *make up* stories to tell her children.

6. **To make up for** means "to compensate for."

> Phil didn't get a very good education in high school, and he's been trying *to make up for* it ever since by reading every book he can get his hands on.

7. **To make up to** means "to get the favor of."

> Bruce thinks he can get ahead in his job by *making up to* the boss, but he'd do a lot better if he did his work more carefully.

many

1. **Many** means "a large number of." It is used with plural count nouns.

56

I've traveled to *many interesting places* and seen *many interesting sights*.

Many letters were missing from the files.

2. While **many** is often used after the verb in affirmative statements, colloquial usage tends to substitute **a lot of** or **lots of** in its place. *I've traveled to many interesting places*, for example, sounds somewhat formal or literary, whereas *I've traveled to a lot of interesting places* sounds more colloquial and conversational. In addition to negative statements, **many** is used in both affirmative and negative questions.

We still have a lot of problems to solve.

We don't have *many problems* to solve now.

Did she get *many job offers* after she graduated?

Has she attended *many schools?*

3. **Many** can be modified by *a good* or *a great*. **A good many** means "a relatively large number"; **a great many** means "a very large number."

There were *a good many students* (relative to the number of students in the class) absent yesterday.

A great many people catch colds or the flu in the winter.

4. **Many** can be used as pronoun.

There were several thundershowers last night. *Many* were very heavy.

She received a lot of job offers. *Many*, however, weren't good enough for her to consider.

5. **Many** can be used as an intensifier with *more* in the comparison of plural count nouns.

We've had *many more rainy days* this year than last.

She has *many more friends* than I do.

mind

1. **Mind** is really several distinct words with different meanings. As a noun, **mind** refers to the quality of intelligence, the brain.

   She's very good in math. She can solve almost any problem in her *mind* without working it out on paper.

   You don't really need to use your *mind* for this job; it's completely automatic.

2. As a verb, one meaning of **mind** is "to take care of."

   I have to go to the store, so you'll have to *mind* the children for an hour or two.

   Whenever I go away, I have to find someone to *mind* my dogs.

3. Another quite different meaning of **mind** as a verb is "to object to, to have an objection to."

   Do you *mind* if I leave early today? (Do you have any objection to my leaving early? Is it all right if I leave early?)

   I *don't mind* if you sit next to me, but I *do mind* if you keep trying to talk to me.

   I *don't* really *mind* hot weather. I really like the heat better than the cold.

4. **Mind** can also mean "to pay attention to."

   Mind that step! You may trip on it.

   You'll have to *mind* your manners when you visit her; she's very formal. (You'll have to pay attention to your manners.)

5. The common expression **never mind** means "don't be concerned."

   "Oh, I'm sorry, I broke your glass!" "*Never mind.* It doesn't matter. I have a lot more glasses."

6. A common colloquial expression is **mind one's own business,** which means "not to interfere, not to be curious about someone else's affairs."

He kept asking me what was in the letter, but I told him to *mind his own business.*

mine   see the entry for *Possessive Forms*

more/most

1. **More** is used for the comparative degree of adjectives, adverbs, and nouns. **More** is generally used with adjectives of more than two syllables, whereas shorter adjectives add *-er* to form the comparative.

His work is *more satisfactory* than we expected.

She finished the exam *more quickly* than I did.

I need *more information* for this report than you've given me.

2. **The most** is used for the superlative degree of adjectives, adverbs, and nouns. Like **more, the most** is generally used with adjectives of more than two syllables, whereas shorter adjectives add *-est* to form the superlative.

She's *the most productive* worker in the office.

I answered the questions *the most accurately* of anyone in the class.

We had *the most rain* last week that we've had all year.

3. **The** is used with **more** in two cases. One is when there is a comparison between two people or things.

She's taking two courses this semester, physics and geometry. Physics is *the more difficult of the two* for her.

Both the blue and the green sweaters cost about the same, but the blue sweater is *the more expensive of the two* by a few cents.

59

4. **The** is also used with **more** in balanced sentences when one comparative is the result of the other.

> *The more work* I do, *the more (work)* there still seems to do.

> That boy always seems to be hungry. *The more* he eats, *the hungrier* he gets.

5. **Most** is used without *the* as an intensifier similar in meaning to **very**, that is, "to a great degree or extent."

> I was *most satisfied* with the results of the interview.

> It was a *most pleasant* evening; we're *most grateful* to you for inviting us.

6. **Most** is also used without *the* with nouns to mean "the largest number or amount of."

> *Most people* are afraid to make mistakes.

> *Most problems* in math are easy for her to solve.

much

1. **Much** means "a large amount or quantity of," and it is used with mass nouns. In conversational usage, **much** seldom occurs in an affirmative statement; **a great deal of, a lot of,** or **lots of** are ordinarily used instead.

> She's done *a lot of work* in the garden this year.
> She hasn't done *much work* in the garden this year.

> He has *a great deal of experience* with computers.
> He doesn't have *much experience* with computers.

2. **Much** is used in both affirmative and negative questions.

> Do we have *much homework* tonight?
> Don't they eat *much bread?*

3. **Much,** like all the words and phrases that express quantity and number, can be used as a pronoun.

> I like ice cream, but I don't eat *much* because I'm afraid of getting fat.

60

4. **Much** is used as an intensifier with the comparative and superlative degree of adjectives and adverbs.

> She's *much happier* in her new job than in her old one.
>
> I was really *much more qualified* for the job than the guy they did hire.
>
> We covered Lesson, Two *much more thoroughly* than Lesson One.
>
> This is *much the most difficult* lesson in book.
>
> I was always *much the shortest* boy in the school.

Note that **much** comes before *the* when it is used with the superlative.

my   see the entry for *Possessive Forms*

n

neither/nor

1. **Neither** and **nor** are negative forms of **either** and **or**. They are most often used to emphasize a negative alternative or choice.

> Martha isn't going *either to the movies or to the party* tonight.
>
> Martha's going *neither to the movies nor to the party* tonight.
>
> *Neither Bill nor Jack* works in a factory.
>
> *Neither the computer nor the photocopier* was working yesterday.

Note that a singular verb form follows **neither . . . nor** when both nouns are singular.

2. Both **neither** and **nor** are used in shortened sentences.

> I didn't get the job, and *neither* did Fred.
> I didn't get the job, *nor* did Fred.
> Helen can't type, and *neither* can Mary.
> Helen can't type, *nor* can Mary.

Note that with both **neither** and **nor** in shortened sentences, the appropriate verb or auxiliary verb comes before the subject.

3. Do NOT use **neither** in colloquial expressions like **Me either.** The negative is already understood with **either,** while **neither** makes a double negative, which is nonstandard usage.

news

News, in spite of the -*s* ending which ordinarily denotes a plural, is a mass noun, singular in form and used with singular verb forms.

All the *news* today *is* good for a change.

There *wasn't* much interesting *news* in the paper this morning.

no

1. **No** is most commonly used as a negative interjection, the opposite of **yes,** in reply to a question or in refusal of a command or request.

"Have you finished the book yet?" "*No*, I haven't."

"It's late. Go to bed now." "*No*. I'm going to stay up and watch the end of this TV program."

2. **No** is also used as an adjective. It is an equivalent of **not any,** though it is frequently more emphatic, about as strong as **not any at all.**

I *have no money*.
I *don't have any money at all*.

There *were no apples* in the store.
There *weren't any apples at all* in the store.

3. **No** is also used as an adjective with the meaning **not a,** though again it is more emphatic than its equivalent.

He's *not a scientist*.
He's *no scientist*. He doesn't understand anything about geology or physics or any subject like that.

I'm *not a typist*.
I'm *no typist*. I just don't pay attention, and I make a lot of mistakes.

4. **No** is also used with the comparative degree of some adjectives and adverbs, again as an equivalent of **not any**.

She's still very sick. She*'s no better* today than yesterday.
She's still very sick. She *isn't any better* today than yesterday.
He*'s no taller* than his father.
He *isn't any taller* than his father.
She *was running no faster* than I was.
She *wasn't running any faster* than I was.

nobody/no one/nothing

1. The **no-** words are among the group known as indefinite pronouns, which refer to unspecified persons or objects or to persons or objects in general. **Nobody** and **no one** refer to persons and are interchangeable; **nothing** refers to objects. Following a verb, they are the equivalents of **not anybody, not anyone,** or **not anything**.

There *wasn't anybody* I knew at the party.
There *was nobody* I knew at the party.
We *haven't found anyone* to fill the job yet.
We*'ve found no one* to fill the job yet.
I *don't have anything* new to report.
I *have nothing* new to report.

2. The **no-** words, both before and after a verb, are the negative forms of the **some-** words.

Somebody answered the telephone.
Nobody answered the telephone.
I *have something* to say to her.
I *have nothing* to say to her.

3. The **no-** words are also the negative forms of the **any-** words in the sense of no matter whom, no matter what.

63

Anyone can solve this problem.
No one can solve this problem.

Anything she decides will be all right with me.
Nothing she decides will be all right with me.

4. As with the other indefinite pronouns, adjectives come after the **no-** words rather than before.

   We've found *no one experienced enough* to fill the job.

   There was *nothing new or interesting* in the report.

5. Because English allows only one negative to a verb, it is necessary to avoid using any other negative with the **no-** words when the meaning is negative. As in math, two negatives in English make a positive, a construction that is not often used.

none (of)

1. **None** means "not one," "not any," or "no amount." It is almost always used in a partitive construction, that is, followed by *of* to indicate a part of a group or a quantity. **None of** can be followed by a plural personal pronoun, a plural count noun, or a mass noun.

   None of us (not one of us) were standing when the bus hit the tree.

   None of the sweaters (not any of them) really look good on me.

   None of this information (no amount of it) is very useful.

2. Traditional grammar would insist on a singular verb after **none,** but modern usage is to follow a plural noun after **none of** with a plural verb form, and a singular noun with a singular verb form.

3. **None of** occasionally occurs after a verb, but this is a rather formal and literary usage; **not any of** would be more common.

   I *earned none of this money.*
   I *didn't earn any of this money.*

64

4. **None of** can be used with a singular count noun when that count noun can be broken down into parts. In this sense, **none of** means "no part of."

> She always has something to do. *None of her day* is ever wasted.
>
> *None of the house* is ever neglected. They keep every bit of it spotless.

nor   see the entry for *neither/nor*

now/nowadays   see the entry for *any more*

O

on

1. For a comparison of **on** with **at** and **in** in place expressions, see the entries for **at** and **in**. In addition, there are a number of common place expressions in which **on** is used.

> The laundry is *on the left* of the supermarket and the drugstore is *on the right*.
>
> The gas station is on *this side* of the street, but the hardware store is *on the other side*.
>
> Their house is *on this street*.
>
> Our apartment is *on the fifth floor*.
>
> There were a lot of passengers *on the bus*.
>
> She wasn't *on the train* she said she'd catch.
>
> The only seat left *on the plane* was in the smoking section.
>
> We took a cruise *on that ship* last winter.
>
> She loves to be *on stage*.
>
> The lighthouse is *on an island* a few miles off the coast.
>
> The children spent the summer *on a farm*.
>
> She won't be in the office this week; she's *on a business trip*.
>
> There isn't anything good *on television* this evening.

2. We sit **on** an armless chair but **in** an armchair. We sit **on** a sofa or a couch.

3. Following are a few more sentences illustrating the uses of **at, in,** and **on** in place expressions.

> There were several people *in the conference room* when I entered.
> The boss was sitting *at the head* of the table.
> There were pads and pencils *on the table.*
> He's *at home* now.
> He's *in his room.*
> He's sitting *on the bed.*
> They spent the summer *in a house on a farm.*
> We were at work *in our office on the sixth floor.*

4. See the entries for **at** and **in** for a comparison with **on** in time expressions. **On** is also used in a few common time expressions.

> They were in San Francisco *on holiday.*
> She didn't know what to do *on her day off.*
> I try to do a lot of different errands *on the same day.*
> The trains almost always arrive *on time.*

Note, however, this special use of *on time.*

> They bought all their kitchen equipment *on time;* they're paying for it in monthly installments.

5. Following are a few more sentences illustrating the uses of **at, in,** and **on** in time expressions.

> I was born *at two o'clock in the afternoon on Sunday* the 30th of May *in 1968.*
> Our class begins *at six o'clock in the evening.*
> I have a job interview *on Friday at nine o'clock in the morning.*
> I like to work *in the morning,* not *at night.*
> There's a holiday *on the second Monday in November.*

66

6. **On** is used in a number of common expressions of manner. Occasionally, these fall into a sort of borderline area between time, place, and manner.

> All the information we need is *on file* in the computer.
>
> The night nurse goes *on duty* at eight o'clock.
>
> The doctor had to leave his telephone number wherever he went because he was *on call.*
>
> We'll leave when all the freight is *on board* the ship.
>
> They didn't know the house was *on fire* because they didn't have a smoke detector.
>
> They had to go to the gas station *on foot* when the car ran out of gas.
>
> He's always *on guard;* he never says anything that gives away his real thoughts.
>
> The potato chips are *on the house;* they're free.
>
> They always keep a large supply of food *on hand* in case of an emergency.
>
> We have that item *on order;* it should be delivered next week.
>
> I think you broke that dish *on purpose;* it wasn't an accident.
>
> That politician never says anything *on the record;* he doesn't like to have his opinions quoted in the newspaper.
>
> There's been a shortage of electricity, but a new generator is coming *on line* next month.
>
> The workers can't decide whether or not to go *on strike.*

one/ones

1. **One** and **ones** are used as pronouns to avoid repeating a noun that has just been mentioned.

> I liked the red sweater, but she liked the green *one* (sweater).
>
> I'm going to buy some new tools. You can have my old *ones* (tools).

2. **One** can be used with *this* and *that,* but **ones** CANNOT be used with *these* and *those.*

I'm going to use this typewriter; you can use *that one* (typewriter).

She likes that house, but I like *this one* (house).

These seats are reserved. You can sit in *the ones* over there.

3. **One** is also used as an impersonal pronoun that is, a pronoun that does not refer to a definite person. It is similar to the impersonal use of **you.**

   You have to stand up for *your* rights.
   One has to stand up for *one's* rights.

   You must study hard to get the most out of the course.
   One must study hard to get the most out of the course.

   This use of *one* is formal and literary.

only

1. **Only** is used as an adjective in the sense of "sole, the one single, unique."

   This interview will be your *only chance* to impress them enough to get the job.

   She's the *only owner* of the business. She doesn't have any partners.

   I was the *only person* in the class who could answer the teacher's question.

2. An **only child** is one who has no brothers or sisters.

   Florence had no one to play with at home because she was an *only child.* Her parents never had another child.

3. As an adverb, **only** is a high-frequency word. It has the general sense of "no more than, no other than."

   She's going to visit *only her sisters* this summer. (She's going to visit no other person.)

   I can meet you *only at seven o'clock.* (I can meet you at no other time.)

George boasts a lot about his job, but he's *only a typist*. (He's no more than a typist.)

We didn't have much time in New York. We got to see *only the Empire State Building*. (We saw nothing more than the Empire State Building.)

I can't go out to dinner with you tonight. I have *only five dollars* in my pocket. (I have no more than five dollars.)

Note that **only,** in the sentences above, occurs immediately before the word or phrase that it modifies. This is considered the correct usage, but in ordinary conversation **only** would be placed with the verb.

She's *only going* to visit her sister this summer.

I can *only meet* you at seven o'clock.

We *only got* to see the Empire State Building.

I *only have* five dollars in my pocket.

4. **Only** can also mean "simply or clearly, without argument or dispute."

If you'd *only agree with me*, we could solve all our differences right now.

If she'd *only speak to me*, I'd know what I did wrong.

5. **Only** is used colloquially as a conjunction with the same meaning as **but;** that is, to connect clauses with contrasting ideas.

I wanted to go out with my friends, *only* I didn't have any money.

6. Equal grammatical elements (two subjects, two objects, two verbs, two clauses) can be connected by **not only . . . but also.** In effect, this is a more emphatic—and more formal or literary—way of saying **and also** or **and . . . too.**

She's *beautiful and smart too*.
She's *not only beautiful but also smart*.
He says he's a vegetarian, but he eats *chicken and also fish*.
He says he's a vegetarian, but he eats *not only chicken but also fish*.

69

His book *made a lot of money and also won a literary prize.*
Not only did his book make a lot of money but it also won a literary prize.

Note that when *not only* begins the sentence, the appropriate verb or auxiliary verb comes before the subject.

Not only is she beautiful *but she's also* smart.

other/others

1. **Other** is used either as an adjective or a pronoun. One meaning is "the remaining one or ones of two or more people or things."

   She took three books out of the library. She returned two of them yesterday, but she hadn't finished *the other one.*

   I was on time, but all *the other students* were late.

   I've seen all but one of those movies; I'll see *the other* next week.

2. **Other** can also mean "different from."

   I wouldn't want to live in *any other city* than this.

   I can't meet you on Thursday. *Any other day* will be all right.

   Note that **other** can be followed by *than.*

3. **Others,** in contrast to **other,** can be used ONLY as a pronoun. Remember that the only adjectives in English that have a plural form are the demonstratives.

   I've seen some of those movies; I don't know when I'll be able to see *the others.*

   Some of the people in the audience were applauding, but *others* were booing.

   Half of the people in the office will take their vacation in the summer; *the others* will go on vacation in the winter.

over

1. **Over** is a preposition with several meanings. The most common is "at a higher level, above."

   I don't like the new supervisor they've put *over us*.

   There are a lot of trees hanging *over the road*.

   I tried to climb *over the wall*, but I couldn't make it.

2. **Over** can also mean "more than."

   My new sweater cost *over thirty dollars*.

   She works *over forty hours* a week.

   He was going *over seventy* when the police stopped him.

   She bought *over a pound* of strawberries.

   Note that **over** is followed by a number or quantity in this use.

3. Another meaning of **over** is "throughout"; in this use, it is intensified by **all**.

   There are always books *all over his house*.

   We spread the Sunday newspapers *all over the floor*.

4. As an adjective, **over** means "finished" or "past."

   What time will the movie be *over?*

   It'll be *over* by 10 o'clock, so we'll have time to go dancing afterwards.

   She's *over* her fever; her temperature is back to normal today.

   Over can also be intensified by **all** in this sense.

   I can finally relax and take a night off from studying; the final exams are *all over*.

5. As an adverb, **over** is used to intensify or to substitute for **again.**

> The teacher didn't like my composition, so I had to *do it over* (again).
>
> He didn't understand me so I had to *say it over* (again).

The expression **over and over** strengthens the idea of a repeated action.

> The teacher made us repeat the sentences *over and over* (again).
>
> I've written to her *over and over* (again), but she hasn't answered me.

6. **Over** is also used as an intensifier with **here** and **there** to point out more exactly the location indicated.

> Come *over here.* I want you to stand right next to me.
>
> You can hang your coat *over here* by the door.
>
> Her office is *over there.* See? It's the second door on the left.
>
> Will you please bring me the magazine that's *over there* on that table in the corner?

In this use, **over** sometimes occurs alone, with **here** or **there** understood.

> "When can you get here?" "I'll be right *over* (there)."

own

1. **To own** is a verb that means "to possess," usually in a rather legal or financial sense.

> They have two cars. Janet *owns* the station wagon, and Sid *owns* the sports car.
>
> They *own* a farm in addition to their house in the city.
>
> We *don't own* our house; we're just renting it.

2. **Own** is also used to strengthen or emphasize possessive adjective forms. **Own** comes AFTER the possessive form.

> I don't need to borrow your pen. I have one of *my own*.
>
> She used to share an apartment, but now she has *her own place*.
>
> They gave him *his own car* for his sixteenth birthday.

3. **Own** is used in a number of idiomatic phrases. One is **to come into one's own,** "to receive something that one deserves."

> She really *came into her own* after she wrote that report; she got both a raise and a promotion.

4. **To hold one's own** means "to keep one's place or position against opposition or trouble."

> They tried to prove that I was wrong, but I was able *to hold my own* because I had good reasons for my suggestions.

5. **On one's own** means "to be responsible for oneself or to do something without help."

> I've been *on my own* since I was seventeen years old. I've made my own living without any help from anyone.
>
> The children drew all these pictures *on their own*. Their mother didn't help them at all.

p

people/person/persons

1. Even though **people** appears to be singular, it is a plural noun and should be used with plural verbs and pronouns.

> Several *people are applying* for jobs as computer operators.
>
> It was very cold in the theater; all the *people were wearing* their coats.

73

I didn't know any of the *people* at the party; *they were* all strangers to me.

2. When a singular for **people** is needed, the word **person** is used most frequently.

Just about *all the people* in the audience were standing and cheering, but there was *one person* sitting there silently.

3. Note that **person** has its own plural form, **persons**.

We needed only *one person* for the job, but *several persons* applied for it.

per   see the entry for *a/an*

plenty (of)

1. **Plenty of** means "a sufficient or more than sufficient amount or number of." It is somewhat stronger than **enough**, which is similar in meaning. **Plenty of** is used with mass nouns and plural count nouns.

We have *plenty of bread*. You don't need to get any when you go to the store.

There's *plenty of time* to finish the exam. You don't need to hurry.

There are *plenty of chairs* in the room. You don't need to bring in any more.

I looked at *plenty of houses* before I bought this one.

2. Colloquially, **plenty** is used as an intensifier equivalent to **very**, that is, "to a great degree."

The exam was *very hard*. Only about half the class passed. The exam was *plenty hard!* Only about half the class passed.

I worked in the garden all day yesterday, so I was *plenty tired* by dinnertime.

Possessive Forms

1. One possessive form in English is the possessive adjective, which is used before a noun.

Personal Pronouns	Possessive Adjectives
I	my
you	your
he	his
she	her
it	its
we	our
you	your
they	their

2. For many students of English, the possessive adjectives are difficult because they always agree with the possessor rather than the thing possessed.

Tom and Helen are married. He is *her* (Helen's) *husband*. She is *his* (Tom's) *wife*.

Tom and Helen are husband and wife. They have a house. *Their house* (Tom and Helen's) is a long way from the city.

Tom and Helen have two cars. They kept *their cars* (Tom and Helen's) in *their* (Tom and Helen's) *garage*.

Tom and Helen are married. They have two children. *Their children* (Tom and Helen's) go to an elementary school.

Tom and Helen are married. I know them well. They are *my friends*.

Tom is *your friend;* Helen is *my friend*.

Tom and Helen are *our friends*. We see them quite often. We go to *their house* (Tom and Helen's) for dinner about once a month, and they come to *our house* pretty often too.

Our school is going to mark *its fiftieth anniversary* with an impressive ceremony.

The company has just revised *its personnel policies*.

3. The idea of possession can be strengthened by the use of **own** after the possessive adjective.

My own car was being repaired, so I had to rent a car.

She needs *her own car* now that she's working again.

They've been renting an apartment. but they're going to buy *a house of their own* this spring.

4. In addition to the adjective forms, there are also possessive pronoun forms.

Possessive Adjectives	Possessive Pronouns
my	mine
your	yours
his	his
her	hers
its	————
our	ours
your	yours
their	theirs

Like the possessive adjectives, the possessive pronouns agree with the possessor, not with the thing possessed. Note also that there is no pronoun form for *its*. In addition, note that an apostrophe (') is NOT used with the possessive pronoun forms.

I had to rent a car because *mine* was being repaired.

My typewriter was broken, but Tom's was okay, so I used *his* to type my report.

Sara and I live in the same apartment building. My apartment is on the third floor and *hers* is on the fifth.

You've met all of my friends, but I haven't met any of *yours*.

We've had dinner at their house, but they haven't had dinner at *ours* yet.

We showed them the pictures we took on our vacation, but we haven't seen *theirs* yet.

5. The possessive of singular nouns is formed by adding -'s to the noun.

This is *Mary's coat;* mine is on the chair over there.

The *company's top executives* all have cars assigned to them.

This is his *secretary's desk.*

6. It used to be taught that nouns ending in -*s* could form the possessive simply by adding the apostrophe ('). Modern usage, however, prefers -'s even with nouns ending in -*s*, except for names from classical antiquity *(Achilles' shield,* for example).

    Charles's hat is on the chair over there.

    Dickens's books are the most popular novels ever written.

7. The possessive form of nouns is used not only with names, organizations, and words such as *man, woman, boy, girl,* and so on, but also with time expressions.

    He spent his whole *month's pay* in one big shopping spree.

    I still have more than a *week's work* on this project.

    Today's news hasn't been very good.

8. Plural nouns that end in -*s* form the possessive simply by adding an apostrophe (').

    The teacher goes over the *students' notebooks* very carefully.

    There are always a lot of cars in front of the *Johnsons' house.*

    The *word processors' work stations* are all in this one large office.

9. The common irregular nouns *(people, men, women,* and *children)* form the possessive in the same way as singular nouns, that is, by adding -'s.

    That candidate is the *people's choice.*

    This is the *children's room;* their parents' room is across the hall.

    She wanted to join the *women's club* because they always had a lot of interesting speakers.

77

pretty

1. As an adjective, **pretty** means "attractive," usually in a sweet or pleasing way.

   Her new *curtains* are very *pretty*. They'll look nice with all the soft colors in her room.

   Everybody says that I was a very *pretty baby*, but I'm not especially handsome now.

   They have a very *pretty house*, with a lot of flowers and trees all around it.

   She has *pretty manners;* she's always sweet and polite to everyone.

   Note, however, that **pretty** can also be used to mean "good or nice" but in an ironical sense.

   That's a *pretty mess!* Now who's going to clean it up?

2. As an intensifier, **pretty** usually means "to a certain degree or extent." It is similar to **somewhat** or **rather.**

   The movie was *pretty good*, but there were parts that were too slow for me.

   I did *pretty well* on the exam; at least I passed it.

   Steve was driving *pretty fast*, but he didn't think he deserved a ticket for speeding.

3. **Pretty,** however, can show a greater degree of intensity, usually with the sense of "more or better than expected." In this sense, it is often used in an exclamatory sentence.

   That was a *pretty good* throw! I didn't think you were such a good ballplayer.

   Hey, that's a *pretty nice* car! When did you get it?

q

quite

1. **Quite** is an intensifier that means "completely, entirely wholly."

   At first we didn't agree with him, but when we read his report, we saw that he was *quite right.*

   It's already noon. You've had *quite enough* sleep now.

   I haven't *quite finished* the book. I still have about twenty pages to read.

2. In this same sense, **quite** or **quite so** can be used as an emphatic affirmative. This usage is more common in British than in American usage.

   "We have all the information we need, don't we?" *"Quite."*

   "Do you agree with me that she's the right person for the job?" *"Quite so."*

3. In a closely related meaning, **quite** can have the sense of "really" or "truly."

   We had *quite a wonderful time* at the party.

   He isn't *quite as smart* as he thinks he is.

   Lynn's taken on *quite an ambitious load* of work at the office.

4. Colloquially, **quite** is used to mean "to a considerable (but not great) extent." In this sense, it weakens its adjective or adverb to some degree.

   Yes, she's *quite pretty*, but I think her sister is much prettier.

   The movie was *quite good*, but I wasn't really all that enthusiastic about it.

5. **Quite** is used as an intensifier with **a lot (of)** and **a few.**

"Do you read much?" "Yes, *quite a lot.*"

You don't need to hurry. We still have *quite a lot of time* before the show begins.

Quite a few people left before the show was over. I guess they didn't like it.

r

rarely   see the entry for *seldom*

rather

1. One use of **rather** is as an intensifier with adjectives and adverbs. It means "to a certain degree, a little." Instead of strengthening its adjective or adverb, **rather** generally weakens it.

    It was *rather hot* yesterday, but not really hot enough to be uncomfortable.

    I did *rather well* on the exam. At least I didn't fail.

    The movie was *rather good*, but I wouldn't want to see it again.

2. **Rather,** usually preceded by **or,** is also used in the sense of "more accurately."

    He was brought up by his mother, *or rather his step-mother;* his own mother died when he was very young, and so it was his father's second wife who raised him.

3. **Rather than** means "in preference to."

    I'll have the French fries *rather than the baked potato.*

    She decided to take algebra *rather than chemistry* this semester.

    She drinks tea in the morning *rather than coffee.*

4. The verb phrase **would rather** also indicates the idea of preference, doing something that is more desirable than an alternative.

> *I'd rather stay home* tonight; there are some good programs on TV.
>
> *She'd rather work for a big company* than a small one.
>
> *He'd rather eat out* all the time than try to cook for himself.

Relative Pronouns

1. The relative pronouns are **who, whom, whose, which, that, when,** and **where.** They introduce adjective clauses; that is, clauses that modify a noun. Adjective clauses follow the noun they modify.

> They're trying to find *the person who is best qualified* for the job.
>
> *The job which they're trying to fill* requires someone with special skills.

2. **Who, whom,** and **whose** refer to people. **Who** is the subject of the verb in the clause; **whom** is the object of the verb in the clause or of a preposition; and **whose** is a possessive form.

> The man *who interviewed me* was the personnel manager himself.
>
> The woman *whom they're interviewing now* appears to be very well qualified.
>
> They don't think the man *whose resumé they just looked at* can do the job.
>
> I don't know all the young people *who are going to the party*.
>
> I don't know all the young people *with whom my daughter is going to the party*.
>
> I do know the boy *in whose car they're going*.

3. **Whom** is an unusual form for English since it usually comes before a verb (or a preposition) rather than after as in normal English word order. Therefore, it is seldom used in daily conversation; **who,** or sometimes **that,** is used instead.

> We didn't know all the people *whom we met* at the party.
> We didn't know all the people *who we met* at the party.
> We didn't know all the people *that we met* at the party.
>
> I can't see the man *to whom she's talking.*
> I can't see the man *who she's talking to.*
> I can't see the man *that she's talking to.*

Note, however, that the use of **whom** is still customary directly after a preposition.

> I can't see the man *to whom* she's talking.
>
> That's the boy *with whom* my daughter is going to the party.

4. **Which** refers to things. It is the subject or object of the verb in the clause or of a preposition. **That** can be substituted freely for **which** except after a preposition.

> I didn't like the book *which I got out* of the library last week.
> I didn't like the book *that I got out* of the library last week.
>
> He's been reading the book *which is* on the desk.
> He's been reading the book *that's* on his desk.
>
> They liked the car *which they looked at* yesterday.
> They liked the car *that they looked at* yesterday.

Note, however, that **which,** like **whom,** is still customarily used directly after a preposition.

> He isn't doing the kind of work *for which* he was trained.

5. As noted, **that** can be substituted for **whom** or **which** except after a preposition. Occasionally in conversation, **that** is also substituted for **who** as the subject, but this is a usage which is considered nonstandard.

6. **Where** is used as a relative pronoun as a substitute for a prepositional phrase (**at which, in which,** and so on) referring to place.

> This is *the office in which* she'll be working.
> This is *the office where* she'll be working.
>
> This is *the house in which* I lived for several years.
> This is *the house where* I lived for several years.
>
> They liked *the hotel at which* they stayed during the convention.
> They liked *the hotel where* they stayed during the convention.

7. **When** is used as a relative pronoun as a substitute for a prepositional phrase (**in which, on which,** and so on) referring to time.

> I'll always remember *the day on which* I graduated from high school.
> I'll always remember *the day when* I graduated from high school.
>
> I always seem to call him on *a day on which* he's out of town.
> I always seem to call him on *a day when* he's out of town.
>
> She had to work very hard during *the years in which* she was starting her career.
> She had to work very hard during *the years when* she was starting her career.

the rest (of)

1. **The rest of** means "the remainder of, what or who is left." It is used with mass nouns or plural count nouns.

> Don't drink *the rest of the milk;* we need it for the children.
>
> Have you read *the rest of these books?* I want to take them back to the library today.
>
> Some of the children are out in the playground, but *the rest of them* are taking a nap.

2. **The rest** (without *of*) is used as a pronoun.

> These are the important sentences. You don't need to bother with *the rest*.
>
> Half of the students have finished the exam, but *the rest* are still working on it.
>
> There's a lot of food left over. I can freeze some of it, but I'll have to throw away *the rest*.

3. **The rest of** can be used with singular count nouns when the count noun can be broken down into parts.

> The windshield was smashed, but *the rest of the car* was undamaged.
>
> I liked the first two or three chapters, but I couldn't read *the rest of the book*.

right

1. **Right** is an adjective with the general sense of "correct, just, suitable," and other related meanings.

> I had the *right answer*, but yours was wrong.
>
> Everybody believed that the judge's *decision was right;* they believed that justice had been done.
>
> That *hat is just right* for you! It looks perfect on you.

2. **Right,** of course, also refers to the right hand—always the speaker's right.

> She's ambidextrous; she can use either her *right* hand or her left to do anything.
>
> When you get to the corner, turn *right,* and then you'll see my house on the left.

3. A **right angle** is a 90° angle formed when one line is perpendicular to another.

> The streets of the city are laid out in a grid so that all the corners are *at right angles.*

4. As a noun, **right** means "a condition that belongs to someone by law or nature."

> If you're arrested, you have a *right* to a lawyer.
>
> You have to stand up for your *rights*. If you don't, people will walk all over you.

> A **right** is stronger than a **privilege.** A right belongs to one by law or nature, but a privilege is granted to one and can be taken away.

5. In politics, **right** (often with **the**) is used to refer to a conservative position.

> In the last election, *the right* won by a large margin, so we can expect more conservative policies from now on.

6. As an adverb, **right** means "straight, directly."

> *Go right to school*, don't stop anywhere on the way.
>
> The children always *come right home* after school.

7. **Right away** means "immediately." (In British usage, the expression **straight away** has the same meaning.)

> You have to start on your homework *right away*, and I mean now, not ten minutes from now.
>
> You'd better hurry, the boss wants to see you *right away*.

8. **Right** is used as an intensifier with **now** and with **here, there,** and other place expressions. It has the sense of "immediately, exactly."

> They're ready to start the meeting *right now*.
>
> I'm not going out. I'll be *right here* all evening.
>
> The telephone is *right over there*. Can't you see it? *Right there* where I'm pointing.
>
> I'll meet you *right in front of* the theater.
>
> The mailbox is *right next to* the elevator.

S

the same

1. **Same** means "identical to, exactly alike."

   We eat dinner at *the same time* every evening, always at seven o'clock.

   She was wearing *the same dress* as another girl; the dresses were exactly alike in every detail.

   My friend and I are taking *the same courses* at school this year, so we're in *the same classes* all the time.

2. **Same** is almost always preceded by **the,** but it can also be used with **this** or **that.**

   It's three o'clock. We leave school at *this same hour* every afternoon.

   It was my birthday, and on *that same day* I graduated from college.

3. **The same** can also be used as a pronoun.

   "I'm having the steak tonight." "Yes, I'll have *the same.*"

4. **The same** is also used as an adverb, often followed by **way.**

   You have to *do this job the same (way)* every time.

say

1. **Say** has the general meaning of "expressing an idea or thought in spoken words." It is used most frequently to introduce a direct or indirect quotation.

   "I'm going to take my vacation in July," she *said.*

   Kim *said* that she was going to take her vacation in July.

   Bert always *says* that he can handle any problem that comes up.

86

2. **Say** and **tell** have the same general meaning when used with direct or indirect quotations, but **tell** must be followed by a noun or pronoun indicating the person addressed.

> "There's nothing wrong with this machine," the repairman *told me*.
>
> She *told her friend* that she couldn't go out that night.
>
> I *told the librarian* that I'd lost the book.

3. With **say,** the person addressed is preceded by **to.**

> He'd lost the book; that's what he *said to the librarian*.
>
> I can never think of anything to *say to her*.

4. **Say** is sometimes used to indicate a guess or estimate.

> There were, *say, a hundred people* in the room.

5. **Say** is also occasionally used as an interjection like **oh, well,** or other words that are not grammatically part of the sentence.

> *Say,* whatever happened to that college roommate of yours?

scarcely   see the entry for *hardly*

seldom

1. **Seldom** is an adverb of frequency; that is, one of the adverbs that answers the question *How often?* **Seldom** means "not often," and it is therefore a negative and should not be used with another negative such as *no* or *not.*

> Kate *seldom drives to work*. (She doesn't drive to work very often.)
>
> I *seldom watch television,* but I do like to see the football games in the fall. (I don't watch television very often.)

87

2. Not quite as common as **seldom** is **rarely,** another negative adverb of frequency that means "almost never."

> I *rarely have any reason* to go into the city these days. (I almost never have a reason to go into the city.)

several

1. **Several** is another word that indicates number, in this case more than two but not many. It is used with plural count nouns.

> The plane was *several minutes* late. It was scheduled to arrive at 4:15, but it didn't get in until 4:25.
>
> It's the time of the year when there's a lot of flu around. *Several employees* were absent yesterday, four or five anyway.
>
> She took *several books* out of the library; she had six or seven or so under her arm.
>
> The teacher likes to give short quizzes. We've had *several* already this month, three or four, I think.

Note that **several,** like all the quantity and number words, can be used as a pronoun, as in the last sentence above.

2. **Several** can be used as an intensifier with **more** and **fewer** when they are followed by plural count nouns.

> There were *several more employees* absent today than yesterday.
>
> I bought *several fewer videotapes* than my friends did.

since see the entry for *for/since*

so

1. One of the principal uses of **so** is to introduce a clause that is the result of a previous clause. **So** is often preceded by **and.**

88

It was a holiday, *so* we were home from work.

My alarm didn't go off this morning, *so* I was late to work.

I couldn't get to the library on Friday when my books were due, *and so* I had to pay a fine the day I did return them.

2. **So** is also used to introduce clauses of result after adjectives and adverbs. The introductory **that** can be omitted.

It was *so cold (that)* I stayed home all day.

She's *so talented (that)* she can do just about anything.

I worked *so hard (that)* I had to go to bed early.

He was driving *so fast (that)* I was scared.

3. This use of **so** is especially frequent with words that indicate number or quantity.

So many people attended the lecture (that) there weren't enough chairs for everyone.

So few people came to the lecture (that) it had to be canceled.

We allowed *so little* time to catch the plane (that) we missed it.

We've had *so much* rain this year (that) everything in the house is damp.

For clauses of result after nouns, see the entry for **such.**

4. **So that** is used to introduce clauses of purpose. The introductory **that** can be omitted.

We left work early *so (that)* we could catch our plane (in order to catch our plane).

They practice every afternoon *so (that)* they'll be ready for the game (in order to be ready for the game).

We stayed home last night *so (that)* we could watch our favorite TV program (in order to watch our favorite TV program).

5. Colloquially, **so as** is used to introduce an infinitive of purpose.

89

They got to the theater early *so as to make sure* they had good seats.

I pretended to be sick *so as to take a day off* from work.

See the entry for **as** for more examples.

6. It used to be taught that in a negative sentence, **so . . . as** instead of **as . . . as** should be used in comparisons of equality. Nowadays, this use occurs rarely in conversation and only occasionally in writing.

   There, you see? The interview was*n't so hard as* you expected!

7. One of the most important uses of **so** is as an affirmative pronoun to substitute for a noun clause after verbs like *think, say, believe, hope,* and so on.

   "Is it going to clear up enough for our picnic tomorrow?" "I *hope so.*"

   "Did she make an appointment to see her doctor?" "I *think so.*"

   "Is there a holiday next week?" "I *believe so.*"

   "Did she do well in the interview?" "The personnel manager *said so.*"

   Note that the negative for **so** in this use is **not.**

   "Is it going to snow tomorrow?" "I *hope not.*"

   "Do you want to go to the movies with us tonight?" "I *think not.*"

8. Another frequent use of **so** is in the expressions **and so on** and **and so forth,** which indicate more of or the rest of items similar to those which have been named. These expressions are equivalents of the Latin phrase **et cetera,** usually abbreviated **etc.**

   We visited several of the most important cities in Europe last summer. You know, Paris, London, Rome, *and so on.*

   We need more office supplies—typing paper, envelopes, typewriter ribbons, paper clips, *and so forth.*

The required courses are English, math, social sciences, *and so on.*

The parts of speech are nouns, verbs, adjectives, pronouns, *and so forth.*

9. **So,** like **too,** is used in shortened sentences in the sense of "in addition."

I worked in the garden yesterday, and *so* did Helen.
I worked in the garden yesterday, and Helen did *too.*

She's looked at these magazines, and *so* has her brother.
She's looked at these magazines, and her brother has *too.*

I took my vacation in July, and *so* did my friend.
I took my vacation in July, and my friend did *too.*

Note that after **so** the appropriate verb or auxiliary verb occurs before the subject.

10. **So** can be used as an intensifier with adjectives or adverbs with the sense of "to a great degree or extent." In this use, **so** is similar to **very,** but **so** often implies a result even when it is not stated. **So** as an intensifier often occurs in exclamatory sentences and in questions.

I was *so tired* this morning! I just couldn't get up when the alarm clock rang.

That movie was *so bad!* We didn't stay till the end.

He drives *so fast!* I'm always afraid when I'm in the car with him.

Why are you *so happy* today?

Why did it take you *so long* to call me?

See also the entries for **too** and **very** for more examples of the use of **so** as an intensifier.

11. **So** can be used alone to mean "very much." Again, it often occurs in an exclamatory sentence in this usage.

He *so* wants to meet you!

She would *so* like to get that job!

91

12. **So** is also used to mean "in the manner or way shown or explained."

> You have to hold your fingers *so* to play the piano.
>
> You must press the keys exactly *so*, or you'll make a mistake.
>
> She always does her work just *so*.

13. **So** also is used as an emphatic contradiction to a previous negative.

> "You can't go out. You didn't do your homework." "I did *so* do it!"
>
> "We're getting ready to go to the movies. It's too bad you don't want to go." "I do *so* want to go!"

14. The phrase **or so** means "more or less."

> Dinner for two will cost fifty dollars *or so* at that restaurant.
>
> I'll be able to leave the office at five o'clock *or so*.

15. **So** by itself can be used as an exclamatory interjection that can express a wide variety of feelings from simple understanding to approval or even disapproval.

> "I've decided not to go back to school next year." "*So!*"
>
> "*So!* It was you who called while I was out."

16. **So what?** is a rather impolite expression, but one that occurs frequently. It means that a previous statement is of no importance.

> "I didn't like the movie." "*So what?* I'm going to see it anyway."
>
> "I'm going to stay home tonight." "*So what?* We'll go without you."

17. **So-so**, also written **so so**, is an expression which indicates that something is not very good, only fair.

"How do you feel today?" "Only *so-so*. I still have a headache, and my nose is running."

"Do you watch much television?" "No, not much. I find that most of the programs are just *so-so*."

some

1. **Some** has a function similar to the indefinite articles **a** and **an** in introducing a previously unidentified or unspecified noun. **A** and **an** are used with singular count nouns *(chair, flower, dish)*, whereas **some** is used with plural count nouns *(chairs, flowers, dishes)* or with mass nouns *(milk, mud, information)*.

   We need *a chair* in this room.
   We need *some chairs* in this room.

   He picked *a flower* to give her.
   He picked *some flowers* to give her.

   I broke *a dish* yesterday.
   I broke *some dishes* yesterday.

   Don't forget to get *some milk* when you go to the store.

   The dog got *some mud* on the floor.

   She wants to get *some information* about computer languages.

2. **Some** is also used as a pronoun with the same general meaning of "an indefinite number or amount."

   "There aren't enough chairs in here for everyone." "Yes, I see. I'll go get *some*."

   "Do you want *some coffee?*" "Oh, no thanks. I've already had *some*."

3. **Some** is used in affirmative statements, whereas, **any** is used in negative statements.

   We need *some chairs* in this corner.
   We don't need *any chairs* in this corner.

   The dog got *some mud* on the floor.
   The cat didn't get *any mud* on the floor.

93

4. Either **some** or **any** can be used in both affirmative and negative questions.

> Are there *some cups* in the dishwasher?
> Are there *any cups* in the dishwasher?
>
> Isn't there *some paper* in the desk?
> Isn't there *any paper* in the desk?

5. **Some of** is used in affirmative statements to indicate a part of an indefinite number or amount. **Any of** in corresponding negative statements indicates none of or not one of the nouns given.

> Put *some of those chairs* in the corner.
> Don't put *any of those chairs* in the corner.

6. **Some** can be used with any class of nouns (singular or plural count nouns, mass nouns) in the sense of unknown, unspecified.

> It's a monument to *some famous man,* but I don't know exactly who he was.
> *Some employees* are going to get additional training.
> *Some information* about the accident appeared in the press.

7. **Some** can be used with numbers to express the idea of approximately, more or less, about.

> *Some fifty people* attended her lecture.

8. Colloquially, **some** is used in the sense of unusual or notable.

> That was *some* party last night! I've never had such a good time.

9. Another colloquial use of **some** is to indicate a great rate of speed.

> You'll have to work *some* to finish all those reports piled up on your desk.

94

somebody/someone/something

1. The **some-** words, like the **any-** and **no-** words, are among the group known as indefinite pronouns, which refer to unspecified persons and objects in general. **Somebody** and **someone** refer to persons and are interchangeable; **something** refers to objects. Remember that the **some-** words are used after verbs in affirmative statements, whereas the **any-** words are used in negative statements.

   There's *somebody* at the door.
   There isn't *anybody* at the door.

   I need *someone* to help me.
   I don't need *anyone* to help me.

   We have *something* interesting to do this afternoon.
   We don't have *anything* interesting to do this afternoon.

2. Before verbs, the corresponding **no-** words act as negatives for the **some-** words.

   Someone knocked at the door.
   No one knocked at the door.

   Something went wrong with the experiment.
   Nothing went wrong with the experiment.

3. Remember that adjectives follow rather than come before the indefinite pronouns.

   She has *something important* to do at the office.
   We need *somebody experienced* to fill this job.

sometime/sometimes

1. **Sometime,** or **some time** as it is often written, means "at an indefinite or unspecified time."

   I want to see you again *sometime soon*, but I can't say exactly when right now.
   Their flight will arrive *sometime on Thursday afternoon*.
   We'll have a dance *sometime next week*.

95

2. **Sometimes** is a quite different word. It refers to the frequency of an action and means "occasionally, now and then."

> We *sometimes* see each other at the office but not too often.
>
> *Sometimes* I'm late to work because I forget to set my alarm clock when I go to bed.
>
> *Sometimes* they spend summer in the mountains and *sometimes* at the seashore.

somewhat

Somewhat is used as an intensifier with adjectives and adverbs to mean "to a certain degree, a little." It is similar in meaning in this sense to **rather**. Instead of strengthening its adjective or adverb, **somewhat** weakens it.

> It's *somewhat cold* this morning, but not cold enough for a heavy overcoat.
>
> I was *somewhat anxious* about the exams, but I was pretty sure I'd pass them even if I didn't get the best grades.

sort of

see the entry for *kind of/sort of*

still

1. For the affirmative and negative distribution of **still** and **any more,** see the entry for **any more.**

2. **Still** is also an adjective that means "silent" or "motionless."

> I was absolutely *still*. I didn't move a muscle, I didn't make a sound.

3. **Still** is also an equivalent of **even** as an intensifier with the comparative.

> When I told him to slow down, he began driving *still faster*.
>
> The final exam was *still more difficult* than the midterm.

4. **Still** is also used as a sentence connector with a meaning equivalent to **nevertheless**.

> I'm not very good in math; *still*, I have to take courses in geometry and algebra to get my degree.

such

1. As we have noted, **so** is used with adjectives and adverbs to introduce clauses of result. With nouns, **such** is used instead of **so** to introduce these clauses. The introductory **that** can be omitted.

> We were having *such a good time* at the party *(that)* we didn't want to go home.
>
> I was reading *such an exciting book (that)* I couldn't put it down.
>
> He's *such a clown (that)* he always makes everyone laugh.
>
> She's *such a musician (that)* it's a pleasure to listen to her play.

Note that when the noun is modified by an adjective, it is possible to shift the pattern to use **so** with the adjective.

> We were having *so good a time* at the party *(that)* we didn't want to go home.
>
> I was reading *so exciting a book (that)* I couldn't put it down.

2. **Such** is often used before a noun when the result is implied but not stated. In effect, the meaning of **such** in these sentences is "to a great extent." The sentences are often exclamatory, with the stress falling on **such**.

> He's *such a clown!*
> We had *such a good time!*
> She's *such a wonderful singer!*
> It's *such a beautiful day!*

3. A basic meaning of **such** is "of that kind."

97

Everything went wrong yesterday. I've never had *such a day* (a day of that kind) before.

They're looking for someone who can handle all their correspondence, but it's going to be difficult to find *such a person* (a person of that kind).

He's dreaming of a job where he'll make a lot of money and not work very hard, but *such jobs* (jobs of that kind) don't really exist.

I'm always looking for places to eat where the food is good and the prices reasonable, but there aren't many *such restaurants* (many restaurants of that kind) around.

4. **Such** and its noun are often followed by a clause beginning with **as,** which limits the meaning of the noun.

Tim's not good at thinking ahead. He seldom follows through on *such plans as* he does make.

Joanne's put *such skills as* she does possess to good use.

When we took them around town, we were able to show them *such sights as* they'd never seen before.

Such experience as he has had won't help him in this job.

5. **Such** can also have the sense of "so much, to a great degree or extent."

With *such talent* as a singer, she should be able to have a successful concert career.

He's always on the go, dashing here and there, doing this and that. I've never seen *such energy*.

6. Another related meaning is "similar, of the same kind."

He's good at basketball, football, baseball, and all *such sports*.

Their office trades in stocks, bonds, debentures, and *other such financial instruments*.

Such can be used as a pronoun as well as an adjective in this use.

If you're going to take up painting, you'll need paints, brushes, canvas, and *such*.

7. **Such** can also be used in the sense of "specific but not named."

> When you go on jury duty, you'll be notified to report at *such a place* at *such a time*.
>
> You're making plans for when you get your degree, aren't you? At *such time* you'll be out in the world all on your own.

The somewhat similar expression **such and such** is used in the sense of "undetermined."

> They kept telling me they'd give me a promotion on *such and such a day*, but they never told me which day.
>
> They discussed the possibility of opening a branch store in *such and such a city*, but they never decided exactly on a particular city.

8. **As such** means "by or of itself."

> *Money as such* is not important to her. She wants it only to make life more comfortable.
>
> *His name as such* won't get any special treatment for him.

See the entry for **as** for more examples.

9. **Such as** means "for example" or "similar to."

> She admires the Impressionist painters, *such as* Monet and Degas.
>
> Courses *such as* geometry and physics are required for all engineering students.

See the entry for **as** for more examples.

t

tell

1. **Tell** has the same meaning as **say** when used with direct or indirect quotations. For the structural difference between the two words, see the entry for **say**.

2. For the difference in meaning between **ask** and **tell** in indirect quotation of imperatives (requests and commands), see the entry for **ask**.

3. **Tell** is used in a number of common expressions.

   She always *tells the children a story* at bedtime.

   I can't *tell you all my experiences* when I was in the army; it would take just too long.

   It has been claimed that George Washington never *told a lie*.

   You won't get into trouble if you *tell me the truth*.

   Yes, I broke the lamp, but please *don't tell on me*. If you *tell on me*, I'll get punished.

   Our little girl has just learned how to *tell time*.

4. **Tell** is often used with the meaning of "discern" or "distinguish."

   He's so color blind that he can't *tell* the difference between red and green.

   The twins look so much alike that I can't *tell* them apart.

   I can always *tell* whether she's happy or not.

than

1. **Than** is used after the comparative degree of adjectives, adverbs, and nouns. Note that in English **that** is NOT used in the comparative.

   He's *healthier than* he was now that he's exercising every day.

100

She takes her work *more seriously than* she should.

The teacher gave us *more time* for the exam *than* we needed.

2. **Than** with the comparative is a conjunction, not a preposition. There is a tendency, however, among native speakers of English to use object pronouns (*me, him, them,* and so on) after **than** in shortened sentences. This not quite acceptable usage can be avoided by following a subject pronoun with the appropriate auxiliary verb.

I'm older *than she is*.

Sally likes the movies better *than I do*.

Chris got a better efficiency rating *than I did*.

I've had more experience *than she has*.

that

1. See the entry for **Demonstratives** for the use of **that** as a demonstrative adjective and pronoun.

2. See the entry for **Relative Pronouns** for the use of **that** as a relative pronoun.

3. Like **the, that** is one of the most common words in English. Indeed, it is so common that it can be omitted in many of its uses, especially in conversation and informal writing, so that it will not be used excessively. In addition to the uses cited above, **that** is also used to introduce many types of clauses. One of these is the object clause after verbs such as *say, think, believe, hope,* and so on. This is one of the uses in which **that** can be omitted.

I *hope (that)* I'll be able to see you next week.

She *said (that)* she'd meet me after work.

He *thinks (that)* she has enough experience to qualify for the job.

4. **That** is also used to introduce clauses after adjectives that indicate mental processes or emotions. This is another of the places where **that** can be omitted.

She's *certain (that)* she'll get the job.
I'm *afraid (that)* I won't get a promotion this year.

5. **That** is also used to introduce clauses of result after **so** and **such.** Again, **that** can be omitted in these sentences.

   The children were making *so* much noise *(that)* I couldn't even think.

   She's carrying *such* a load of classes *(that)* she never has time to do anything but study.

6. **That** also introduces clauses of purpose with **so** and again can be omitted.

   I have to work overtime this week *so (that)* I can take some time off next week.

   For more examples of clauses with **that,** see entries for **so** and **such.**

the

1. **The** is perhaps the most frequently used word in English. It is known as the definite article, in contrast to **a** and **an,** the indefinite articles. **The** is used with nouns that have been previously identified or specified.

   He wrote her a letter. When she read *the letter* (in other words, the letter that he wrote her), she was very happy.

2. **The** is sometimes stressed and pronounced like *thee.* Stressed **the** indicates something or someone very special or noteworthy.

   It's *the movie* of the year. You really have to see it.

   That's *the restaurant* where you should go. It's *the most fashionable place* in town.

   She's *the outstanding student* of *the year.* She gets *the best grades* in *the entire school.*

3. **The** is ordinarily not used with the names of people, even when they are preceded by a title of respect.

102

I have an appointment with *Dr. Wilson* tomorrow.

Mrs. Clark is the new office manager.

The voters reelected *Senator Fielding* by a large margin.

Note, however, that **the** can be used with names to avoid confusion or misunderstanding. In this case, the name is usually followed by an identifying clause.

The Mrs. Clark to whom I was talking is the new office manager.

No, no, he's not *the Bill that I met at the party*, he's *the Bill who's in the mailroom at the office.*

4. **The** is also used when names occur in the plural, referring to a married couple or a family.

We're going to have dinner with *the Clarks* next Saturday.

We ran into *the Johnsons* at the shopping mall last Sunday.

their/theirs   see the entry for ***Possessive Forms***

these/this/those   see the entry for ***Demonstratives***

too

1. **Too,** is interchangeable with **also,** and has the meaning of "in addition." **Too,** however, most frequently comes at the end of a sentence, whereas **also** normally occurs before a simple main verb or after the first auxiliary in a verb phrase.

She cleaned the house this morning, and she *also worked* in the garden.

She cleaned the house this morning, and she worked in the garden *too*.

He's studied medicine, and he*'s also taken* some courses in psychology.

He's studied medicine, and he's taken some courses in psychology *too*.

103

2. **Too** sometimes occurs directly after a noun or pronoun to avoid confusion about what is being added to what.

> She's taking chemistry *too*. (Either she's taking chemistry in addition to some other subject, or she's taking it in addition to someone else; only the context would make the meaning clear.)
>
> *She too* (in addition to someone else) is taking chemistry.
>
> She liked the movie, and though I don't always agree with her, *I too* thought it was very good.

3. **Too** in the sense of "in addition" is used in shortened sentences, where it is equivalent of **so** in similar shortened sentences.

> The yard needs cleaning, and the garage does *too*.
> The yard needs cleaning, and *so* does the garage.
>
> Tom has a date tonight, and I do *too*.
> Tom has a date tonight, and *so* do I.
>
> My friends are all going to the dance, and I am *too*.
> My friends are all going to the dance, and *so* am I.

4. **Too** is also used as an intensifier with adjectives and adverbs; that is, it is one of the words like **very** that make the adjective or adverb more (or occasionally less) emphatic. **Too** in this use has the meaning of "in excess."

> We've had *too much snow* this winter, a lot more than we really need.
>
> Algebra was just *too difficult* for me; I had to drop out of the class.
>
> I always keep a stepladder in the kitchen because I'm *too short* to reach the top shelves.
>
> You're walking *too fast!* I can't keep up with you.

5. When **too** intensifies an adjective or adverb, the phrase is often followed by an infinitive.

> He's *too short to be* a good basketball player.
>
> We were held up in traffic, so we were *too late to see* the beginning of the movie.
>
> She takes her work *too seriously to joke* about it.

104

6. Many students of English have difficulty with the difference between **too, very,** and **so** as intensifiers. **Too,** as noted above, means "in excess," whereas **very** means "to a great degree or extent, extremely." **So** implies a result, even when the result is not stated. **So** is often used in exclamatory sentences.

It was *very hot* yesterday. (This is a simple statement that it was extremely hot.)
It was just *too hot* yesterday to do anything at all. (It was excessively hot yesterday.)
It was *so hot* yesterday! I just stayed home all day. (As a result of the heat, I stayed home.)

The exam was *very hard.*
The exam was *too hard* for me; I couldn't finish it.
The exam was *so hard!* I just couldn't finish it.

You're driving *very fast.*
You're driving *too fast.* Slow down before you get a ticket.
Don't drive *so fast!* You're scaring me!

u

used to/be used to/get used to

1. **Used to** is a verb phrase that indicates an action which was habitual or customary or of long duration in the past. It is always followed by the simple form of the verb.

I *used to eat* at that restaurant all the time, but I finally got tired of the food.

She *used to be* a typist, but she went to night school, and now she works as a travel agent.

We *used to live* in this neighborhood, but we moved away a long time ago.

I *used to sleep* late on Saturday and Sunday, but now I get up early every day.

2. **Be used to,** on the other hand, means "to be accustomed to." It is followed either by the *-ing* form of the verb or by a noun.

> He's *used to eating* a big breakfast.
>
> I'm *used to getting up* early every morning.
>
> She *isn't used to the way* we do things in this office.
>
> The students *are used to the quick quizzes* that the teacher gives them.

3. **Get used to** means "to become accustomed to." Like **be used to,** it is followed by the *-ing* form of the verb or by a noun.

> Danny never could *get used to working* at night, so he had to quit his job.
>
> Peggy doesn't want to *get used to watching* television every night.
>
> You'll *get used to the pressure* of the job.
>
> We couldn't *get used to the way* the teacher talked.

V

very

1. Intensifiers are words that strengthen (or occasionally weaken) the adjectives and adverbs with which they are used. **Very** is the most frequently used intensifier and the one usually cited to illustrate this group of words. **Very** means "to a great degree or extent."

> She's a *very capable* worker. She does all her work quickly and correctly.
>
> It was *very hot* today. The temperature was close to 90 degrees.
>
> He takes his school work *very seriously*. He's never absent, he does all his homework, and he spends extra time reading up on his subjects.

106

2. Some students of English confuse **very, too,** and **so** as intensifiers. **Very,** as noted, means "to a great degree or extent"; **too** means "in excess"; and **so** suggests some kind of result, even though the result is not stated.

> It was *very hot* yesterday. (This is a simple statement of fact.)
>
> It was *too hot* to do anything yesterday. (It was excessively hot yesterday.)
>
> It was *so hot* yesterday! I just couldn't do anything. I stayed home all day. (As a result of the heat yesterday, I stayed home all day.)
>
> She's *very serious.* (Again, this is a simple statement of the fact that she's serious to a great degree.)
>
> She's *too serious.* She never has any fun at all. (She's excessively serious.)
>
> She's *so serious!* (A result—she's not any fun to be with, for example—is implied but not stated.)

See the entries for **so** and **too** for more examples of their use as intensifiers.

W

when see the entry for ***Relative Pronouns***

where see the entry for ***Relative Pronouns***

which see the entry for ***Relative Pronouns***

while/a while

1. **While** is a conjunction that introduces time clauses. It indicates that two actions were taking place at the same time.

> I was trying to read *while* my brother was watching television.

107

While we were checking the figures, the supervisor kept looking over our shoulders.

2. **All the while** is more emphatic than **while** alone and indicates that one action continued throughout, or for the entire duration of, the other action.

   All the while we were supposed to be listening to the lecture, we were laughing and joking among ourselves.

3. **While** is also used as a conjunction to indicate a contrast between two clauses. It is an equivalent of **although** or **whereas** in this use.

   Although I had prepared for the interview, I was still very nervous about it.
   While I had prepared for the interview, I was still very nervous about it.
   She buys a lot of books, *whereas* I get them from the library.
   She buys a lot of books, *while* I get them from the library.

4. **While** is also a noun meaning "an indefinite period of time." It is preceded by **a.**

   I still have some work to finish up, so it'll be *a while* before I'm ready to leave.
   They're going to take *a long while* to fix my car.
   The children just ate, so they can't go in the water for *a little while*.

who/whom/whose   see the entry for *Relative Pronouns*

worth/worthy/worthwhile

1. **Worth** is used as both a noun and adjective to indicate the value of a thing or a person in terms of either money or merit. The English expression **to be worth** is the equivalent of a verb in some other languages.

   The paintings in the museum *are worth* several million dollars.

108

It'*ll be worth* your time to visit the museum and look at all the paintings.

It *wasn't worth* the trouble to study for the exam; it was too easy.

She has a big collection of pottery. She says it'll *be worth* a lot of money someday.

2. **Worthy** is an adjective that is used most often in the sense of "deserving." It is frequently followed by a phrase with *of* or by an infinitive.

They're very charitable. They give a lot of money to *worthy causes*.

Her work is certainly *worthy of all the praise* she's received.

He's *worthy to be elected* as our representative.

3. **Worthwhile** is also an adjective. It means "of sufficient value or importance to compensate for effort or time."

Going to the museum wasn't a waste of time. It was very *worthwhile*. We saw a lot of beautiful paintings.

The time and effort you spend on your studies will be *worthwhile*. You'll understand your subjects better and get better grades.

y

yet

1. For the affirmative and negative distribution of **yet** as a time word and **already,** see the entry for **already.**

2. In addition to its use as time word, **yet** (or **and yet**) is an equivalent of **but** to introduce a clause whose meaning contrasts with a previous clause. This use of **yet** is somewhat formal.

His career has been very successful, *yet* he feels he could have done more with his life.

She doesn't have a great deal of experience, *and yet* she expects to get the job.

your/yours   see the entry for ***Possessive Forms***

APPENDIX A

Words with Affirmative and Negative Distribution

Some of these words have special uses in which they may not follow the affirmative-negative pattern. These exceptions are noted in the text.

Affirmative	Negative
already	yet
also	either
some	any
somebody	anybody
someone	anyone
something	anything
someplace	anyplace
somewhere	anywhere
still	any more
a long way	far
a great deal of/ lots of/a lot of	much

APPENDIX B

Words with Count and Mass Noun Distribution

An asterisk (*) denotes a special meaning of the word which is discussed in the text.

Singular Count Nouns	Plural Count Nouns	Mass Nouns
a/an	————	————
all*	all	all
————	any	any
————	————	a bit of
————	a couple of	————
each	————	————
enough*	enough	enough
every	————	————
————	a few/few	————
————	fewer/fewest	————
————	————	a good deal of
————	————	a great deal of
————	————	a little/little
————	————	less/least
————	a lot of	a lot of
————	lots of	lots of
————	many	————
————	a good many	————
————	a great many	————
————	————	much
————	plenty of	plenty of
————	several	————
————	some	some
that	————	that
the	the	the
————	these	————
this	————	this
————	those	————